YOUR LIFE,

YOUR LEGACY II

PROTECTING THE ONES YOU LOVE

Cover design by: Dean Andrade

Layout:
Laura Wilson
Wilson Advisors, LLC
Madison, Wisconsin 53719

Proofreader:
Becky Wilson

Book printing by:
Publisher's ExpressPress
Ladysmith, Wisconsin 54848

Printed in the United States of America
by
Legacy Educational Publishing, LLC
7633 Ganser Way, Suite 100
Madison WI 53719

Authors' Note

This book addresses important estate planning ideas for individuals and business owners. Although it is intended to provide a general introduction to the legal, accounting, tax, financial planning, and investment issues that affect your estate plan, you should not rely upon this book as your sole source of information and advice for these important topics. Changes in the law (or the court's interpretation of the law) occur frequently, and any changes made after this manuscript was completed may affect the recommendations made by the authors. Also, these recommendations are general in nature and therefore may not be suitable for every reader.

A reference book like this one should never be seen as a substitute for professional assistance. Legal, accounting, tax, financial planning, investment, or other advice should be obtained from competent professionals. For your estate planning needs, we recommend that you consult with one of the Legacy Educational Publishing Members listed in this book. These attorneys dedicate their legal practices to working with families to design and implement estate plans that meet each family's individual needs and desires. Your family's situation is unique and should receive individual attention.

Contents

INTRODUCTION

This book is intended to help you understand important estate planning concepts that can greatly benefit you and your family. Its goal is to equip you with the knowledge you need to make informed choices concerning your estate planning options. We believe that this knowledge will allow you to:

- Stay in control of your property throughout your life;

- Implement a plan to carry out your health care desires and pass your instructions concerning the use of your property if you become disabled;

- Distribute your property to whom you want, when you want, and how you want;

- Avoid probate and guardianship court hearings; and

- Help you and your loved ones escape unnecessary taxes, court costs, and professional fees.

Legacy II is a sequel to Your Life, Your Legacy, The Fundamentals of

Estate Planning. While that book addresses many estate planning questions and issues, as its name suggests, it was never intended to provide a comprehensive discussion of every estate planning issue. Following its publication, our readers asked if we could write another book that answers additional and more in-depth estate planning questions. This book is written in response to those requests. Among the many topics covered, it answers the following questions:

- Can my estate plan be written to protect my spouse from lawsuits, creditors, and predators?

- How should I plan for a child with special needs?

- How can I motivate my parents to plan their estate?

- What special estate planning issues exist for singles and unmarried couples?

- What planning is necessary to protect my IRA for my beneficiaries?

- Why is it important that I develop a business succession plan and how can I best implement it?

- How can I best leave a gift to my favorite charity?

- How can I protect my estate from nursing home costs?

If you have ever asked yourself any of the above questions, this book is for you. Its easy-to-understand question and answer format is written by some of this country's leading estate planning attorneys who work daily with families like yours helping them solve their estate planning problems and giving them the peace of mind of knowing that their estates are well protected. If you want that same peace of mind, you owe it to yourself and your loved ones to read this book and learn from them how to best protect yourself, your family, and your estate. After all, it is *Your Life, Your Legacy*!

CHAPTER ONE

BACK TO THE BASICS

THE IMPORTANCE OF UNDERSTANDING THE BASIC CONCEPTS OF ESTATE PLANNING

In Your Life, Your Legacy—The Fundamentals of Effective Estate Planning (or Legacy I), we shared how important it is to take control of the planning of your estate. We defined a good estate plan as one that puts you in charge of your property while you are alive and well, protects you and your loved ones if you become disabled, and allows you to pass on what you have to whom you want, when you want, the way you want, and at the same time minimizes taxes, professional fees, and other costs.

Legacy I starts with a review of the laws pertaining to the ownership of property. It discusses the many problems with wills, including the fact that estates planned with them usually have to undergo the delays, costs, emotional toil, and other significant problems that exist with the probate court process. It is for this reason we recommend that families who want to avoid probate use revocable living trusts as the foundation of their estate plan.

Legacy I also reviews many other basic planning issues including how to best plan ahead for your incapacity or death, the importance of powers of attorney, limited partnerships, charitable planning, asset protection, estate taxation, and multi-generational planning among others. Since these issues are all covered in *Legacy I*, they are not repeated in this book. Anyone needing a refresher course on the fundamentals of effective state planning is encouraged to start by reading *Legacy I* first.

This book begins where *Legacy I* ends. Instead of covering just basic estate planning laws and strategies, *Legacy II—Planning For Those You Love*, delves deeper into the challenges faced by those of us with more complex situations and offers straightforward solutions to those challenges.

Each chapter in this book focuses on a different estate planning topic and is written to stand alone. We encourage you to peruse the Table of Contents to identify those chapters that specifically pertain to you and read them first. This will arm you with the information you need to start planning for the challenges that deserve and require your immediate attention.

Once you have completed those chapters, we encourage you to then finish the rest of the book. The chapters that do not apply to you right now, will often contain valuable information that you will need in the future or may be helpful to your parents, siblings, friends and other loved ones.

Life is complex, and not everyone's planning needs can be met with just basic information and simple strategies. Now more than ever, in order to protect those you love, it is critical that you plan for those you love. This book is written for our readers who face these more complex challenges.

CHAPTER TWO

ESTATE PLANNING WITH TRUSTS

Trusts have been used since the Middle Ages and actually predate wills. Trusts have replaced wills as the estate planning strategy of choice because they provide superior planning opportunities that cannot be accomplished with wills. Trusts are extremely flexible tools that can be used for a wide variety of purposes. Previously used only by the rich, trusts are now for everyone.

In this chapter, we'll go over the most common types of trusts used in estate planning and explain why they are superior to other planning strategies. Trusts can provide many lifetime benefits and protections for those who are wise enough to use them. Wills, on the other hand, never benefit the maker since they are only effective after you die. In other words, it's too late to take advantage!

The instructions you place in your trust keep you in control of your property if you become incapacitated and help your family avoid court-directed guardianship proceedings. Wills offer no such protection. Trusts allow you to eliminate court supervision of the administration of your estate, while wills are your ticket to probate court. Trusts keep your affairs private, but wills are part of the court record and open to public scrutiny.

What is a trust?

To help you gain an intuitive understanding of trusts, let's draw an analogy. Think of a trust as the equivalent to a detailed list of babysitter instructions. Just like no parent entrusts their children to a new babysitter without leaving a detailed set of directions for the sitter to follow, each person who creates a trust (sometimes called a Grantor, Settlor, or Trustmaker) includes a detailed set of instructions that the Trustee (or "babysitter" of your property) is required to follow. These instructions explain to the Trustee what you desire to be done with your property while you are alive and well, when or if you are disabled, and after your death.

A trust is a special contract between the Trustmaker and Trustee for the benefit of the beneficiary. By signing the contract, the Trustee is required to carry out the instructions of the trust.

Although a trust has three distinct roles, it does not require three distinct people. The same person can wear all three hats by establishing the trust (Trustmaker), managing the trust (the Trustee), and also being the beneficiary of the trust. Because of this capability, you have the wonderful opportunity to create, manage, and benefit from your own trust. If you are married, you and your spouse can create, manage, and benefit from a joint trust.

As estate planning attorneys, we find that our clients predominately want to be in control of their assets while they are alive and well, during incapacity, and even after death. The trust is the perfect vehicle to accomplish all of these goals.

As the maker of the trust, you decide:

- Who will control the trust by serving as the initial or successor Trustees.

- Who will manage your property or business after incapacity or death.

- Who will be the initial beneficiaries.

- Who will be the beneficiaries after the death of the initial beneficiaries.

- Your special care instructions if you become disabled.

- Who is allowed to see your trust.

- Investment and management instructions for your property.

- How the trust property will be used for your beneficiaries.

- Whether to include special planning to reduce estate taxes.

- Whether to include special instructions to protect the inheritance from predators and creditors.

- Any other special provisions you want to include.

There are two main types of trusts: living and testamentary. The type of trust you use depends on which of the above goals you want to promote.

What are the differences between living and testamentary trusts?

The principal difference between living and testamentary trusts is when they go into effect. Living trusts go into legal effect immediately upon signing. They are known as inter vivos trusts, which means "during lifetime" in Latin. This distinguishes them from trusts created in wills (testamentary trusts) that do not take legal effect until the maker's death. Like wills, testamentary trusts go through the probate process and are supervised by the court system, while living trusts escape court supervision. Living trusts can technically be either revocable or irrevocable, but the term "living trust" commonly refers only to revocable trusts.

What are the differences between revocable and irrevocable trusts?

A trust may be either revocable or irrevocable. The primary difference between revocable and irrevocable trusts is that revocable trusts can be amended whenever the Trustmaker desires without needing court permission. Revocable trusts are popular because they provide the Trustmaker with maximum flexibility for controlling all the property in the trust plus the ability to change the plan at any time without anyone else's permission. With an irrevocable trust, the Trustmaker may not independently amend the trust without court permission. A trust that does not expressly reserve the power to revoke is considered an irrevocable trust.

Irrevocable trusts are used for special planning goals and are appropriate when the benefits to be achieved outweigh the ability to amend without court permission. Irrevocable trusts may be used in special circumstances to achieve estate and income tax planning goals; protect the estate from nursing home costs; obtain asset protection for beneficiaries; or to plan for persons with special needs. *Ryan*

During the Trustmaker's lifetime, revocable trusts pose no income tax issues because the income and expenses "pass through" to the Trustmaker and are reported on the Trustmaker's personal income tax return. Following the death of the Trustmaker, the trust becomes irrevocable and therefore a separate taxable entity with its own taxpayer identification number.

What instructions should I include in my trust?

Whatever you want! You can tailor your trust instructions to meet your unique needs, as well as those of your loved ones. The more clear, detailed, and specific your instructions, the better your Trustee will be able to understand your desires and fulfill your objectives.

For example, if you want to be cared for in your home if you become disabled, your trust should say so. Your trust should also authorize your Trustee to pay for this type of care. Money will be needed to maintain your home and possibly remodel your home for wheelchair accessibility. You should grant authority to pay for visiting nurses, 24-hour care, hospice, or other needed caregivers to make staying at home possible. If you wish to continue your daily routine to the maximum extent possible, you can include directions for your recreational activities, travel (including travel companions), and religious or spiritual involvement.

Business owners will want to give special instructions for the continued operation, transfer, or liquidation of their business. The instructions need to specify whether the Trustee or someone else will be responsible for implementing these decisions.

Other detailed instructions will allow you to leave what you want, to whom you want, when you want, and in the way you want, just as if you were there personally giving direction. For instance, you can instruct your Trustee to use your estate to care for your children, provide them with quality education, and offer incentives to encourage them to excel in life.

With careful thought, you can creatively plan to benefit friends, relatives, grandchildren, and charities. Your planning can even be designed to benefit them immediately or over a period of many years.

Should I plan with a trust?

To determine if a trust is right for you, simply ask yourself the following questions:

- Do you want your family to pay the expenses of probate, which are often between 3% and 8% of the gross value of an estate (up to $8,000 for a $100,000 estate)? *NO*

- Do you want the publicity involved in a probate where anyone can see what your beneficiaries inherit? *No*

- Do you want your family to suffer the delays of the probate process? *No*

- Do you want a judge to be in charge of settling your estate instead of the Trustee you choose? *No*

- Do you want your money frozen by the court following your death? *NO*

- Do you want your family to go through a probate in each state where you own real estate? *No*

- Do you want intrusive guardianship court proceedings if you become incapacitated? *No*

- Do you want a will contest to take place when you can't defend your actions?

If you answered "No" to any of these questions, then planning with a trust is right for you.

We believe the advantages of a revocable living trust far outweigh the disadvantages.

A well-drafted trust is clearly one of the most beneficial estate planning opportunities available today. By maintaining control over your estate plan, you can decide for yourself the best use of your property and how to benefit and protect yourself and your family.

CHAPTER THREE

PROTECTING YOUR SPOUSE

Planning to protect your surviving spouse after your death can be as important, if not more important, as planning to protect your entire estate. There is always the potential danger of a creditor taking all of your surviving spouse's assets or a predator taking advantage of your surviving spouse. Losses sustained by your spouse also adversely affect your children's inheritance.

What is a creditor?

A creditor can be anyone who demands payment from your spouse for debts or who files a lawsuit against your surviving spouse claiming your spouse is legally liable to them. Litigants might be seeking compensation for slip and fall accidents, automobile crashes, or any of the many other reasons that people are being sued these days. The cost of defending against such litigation and a possible judgment that awards huge damages can financially ruin a surviving spouse which will also impact negatively on your children.

What is a predator?

A predator is anyone who preys upon your surviving spouse for money, including a new suitor. A predator can also be the person who marries your surviving spouse with good intentions, but when the marriage goes bad, initiates a divorce to take as much as he or she can from your spouse. Either way your spouse can be financially wiped out. The good news is that careful planning with the right attorney can protect your surviving spouse from these disastrous situations.

How do I protect my spouse from creditors?

When a spouse dies, the estate is usually left outright to the surviving spouse. This is a big mistake! Anything owned by your surviving spouse can be taken away. The first rule of protecting 1. your spouse from creditors after your death is, "Do not let your spouse own your assets after you die."

Death assets are in the Trust

This strategy is not as bad as it sounds. In fact, most spouses actually appreciate the strategy when they learn they can maintain the benefits of ownership without the risk of having it exposed to any creditor claims.

done To implement this strategy requires that you first create a revocable living trust and transfer your assets into it. When you die, the instructions of your revocable trust state that your assets will be moved to a special trust inside your revocable trust that can be used for your surviving spouse's health, education, maintenance, and support. These instructions mean that all of the trust's assets are available to maintain your spouse's lifestyle. The beauty of this plan is that although your spouse will receive all the benefits of being a trust beneficiary, your spouse will not face any of the risks faced by those who receive their inheritances outright, including the risk of losing it to creditors.

As a trust beneficiary, your spouse is entitled to what the law calls the "beneficial enjoyment" of the trust property. This gives your spouse all of the benefits of enjoying the use of the trust property without fear of losing it to creditors.

This arrangement gives your spouse "control without ownership." Even though the trust owns the assets, your spouse will continue to manage and control them. The benefit is that if a creditor makes a claim against your spouse, assets in the trust are protected because they are not legally owned by your spouse— they are your assets left in trust under your spouse's control and for your spouse's benefit. Because a creditor is not your spouse, the creditor has no right to claim the trust's assets!

Cina can leave the assets in the trust 37% tax

Does every trust protect my spouse from creditors?

No! Not all trusts provide creditor protection. If creditor protection is desired, the trust must be carefully planned and drafted to achieve this valuable benefit. Lawyers with expertise in estate planning will know what provisions are needed to protect your spouse from creditors.

What about protection from predators?

An "Asset Protected Trust" also provides protection from predators. A knowledgeable estate planning attorney will insert special provisions into the trust to keep predators away from your spouse's door. Special trust provisions may include:

- Directions that the trust assets can be used only by your spouse and no one else;

- Appointment of a co-trustee to help protect your spouse from potential predators; and

- A requirement that prior to remarriage the new spouse must sign a prenuptial agreement relinquishing all claims against your spouse's assets.

this

Is a prenuptial agreement really a good idea?

Most estate planning attorneys counsel their clients who are about to remarry to consider putting a prenuptial agreement in place. Essentially, the prenuptial says, "what's mine is mine and what's yours is yours, and should we ever divorce, or if one of us dies, I keep my stuff and you keep yours." This is only fair because if a divorce should occur when the marriage is still young, your surviving spouse will leave the new marriage with the same assets he or she brought into it, as well as an equitable share of any assets acquired together during the marriage.

How can I help my spouse insist upon a prenuptial agreement?

Your trust's directions can provide financial incentives for your spouse to request a prenuptial agreement. For example, your trust instructions can require the trustee to cut off distributions to your spouse if a remarriage occurs without a prenuptial agreement being signed. If a prenuptial agreement is signed, your spouse can still fully use and enjoy the distributions from of the asset protected trust. Your spouse can blame the need for a prenuptial agreement on the terms of the trust, and thereby avoid the difficult discussion of what happens if the marriage fails.

By putting the proper planning in place, you will have the peace of mind of knowing that your spouse (and the future inheritance of your children) will be protected from potential creditors and predators. By the way, you just might be the spouse who survives and is glad to find that these asset protections are in place for your benefit!

YOUR LIFE, YOUR LEGACY II

CHAPTER FOUR

PLANNING FOR LOVED ONES WITH SPECIAL NEEDS

Of all the important estate planning actions to take, perhaps none is more important than planning your estate to protect your loved one with special needs. This is because your loved one is depending on you to have a backup plan in place to protect his or her interests if you are no longer able to protect them yourself.

No one knows better than you do the challenging physical, mental, and emotional issues that must be addressed daily concerning every aspect of your loved one's life. You are involved in supervising living arrangements, medical treatments, dietary needs, education, finances, and eligibility for government benefits for your loved one, to name but a few of the exceptionally important issues that are unique to him or her. Often caregivers like you discover that the emotional, financial, and other costs of providing such required supervision not only continues, but even increases, after a child with special needs becomes an adult with special needs.

You are not alone if you find it difficult to obtain reliable information on how to ensure that the many issues addressed above will be handled properly upon your disability or death. In our experience, the information that exists on these issues is not only scarce, but it is also often conflicting or just plain wrong.

If you find yourself in this troubling situation, you are probably up late at night worrying about your loved one's future and the following questions:

- Who will care for my loved one when I am no longer able to because of my own advanced age, disability, or death?

- Where will my loved one live?

- Who will make medical decisions?

- How will others know of my loved one's daily routine, likes and dislikes, special diets, medications, and other unique needs?

- Who will handle finances and legal issues?

- Will leaving my loved one an inheritance disqualify him from receiving government benefits?

- How can I be sure that in my absence my loved one will have the best opportunity for a happy and fulfilling life?

The good news is that answers to these and many other questions like them is readily available for you. What you need is the professional assistance of an estate planning attorney who understands the critical issues that you face daily. Only an estate planning attorney with experience and empathy can help you navigate the myriad legal, financial, and other challenges of planning for your loved one's future. The plan that you design and implement with the guidance of your estate planning attorney will provide you the peace of mind that comes with knowing the care of your loved one will be handled exactly the way you want.

Where do I start?

Your first step in protecting your loved one is to select a trusted family member or friend to supervise the personal, financial, and legal affairs of your loved one when you are no longer able to handle them. We understand that this selection is difficult, but who is better able to make it than you? Who better understands the unique needs of your loved one? Who knows better which of the potential caregivers will provide the compassionate care and protection that your loved one needs and deserves?

The worst thing you can do is nothing. If you fail to make the appointment yourself, you will leave the selection of your loved one's future caregiver to the mercy of judges and social workers. They are more then ready to select your loved one's caregiver if you fail to chose one yourself. Do you want to choose the caregiver yourself or leave the choice to the intrusive and costly court system?   When made aware of their options, our clients select the caregiver themselves and take the steps necessary to make their wishes legally binding.

How can I make my selection legally binding?

Every state has a legal process to appoint individuals (known as guardians) to handle the affairs of children or adults who are incapable of taking care of themselves. Parents of a child with special needs can designate a guardian in their Will. In the case of an adult with special needs, the guardian who is currently serving can request a judge to appoint a successor guardian to take over when needed. The successor guardian will have the legal right to handle the health care and financial affairs of your loved one.

What if I want different individuals to handle the health care and financial affairs of my loved one?

You know that the skills required to supervise the health care needs of your loved one are vastly different from those needed to manage his or her finances. The individual who is best qualified to tuck your loved one in at night and make medical decisions might be the least qualified to handle financial or legal issues (and vice versa). The first responsibility (housing and health care) requires someone with a "good heart" who is loving and understanding. The law calls this individual the "guardian of the person" because this guardian oversees personal care needs.

The second responsibility (financial and legal) requires someone with "a good head on his or her shoulders." Such a person must possess sound financial and legal judgment. The law calls this person the "guardian of the estate" because this guardian oversees financial and legal issues.

You are fortunate if you know someone who is equally qualified to serve as both a guardian of the person and of the estate for your loved one. If not, there is no need to worry because the law allows you to name different individuals for these very different roles. Any good plan to provide for the future care of your loved one starts with resolving these guardianship issues. Once the proper guardians are selected, it is necessary to provide them specific written instructions concerning the proper care desired for your loved one.

What kinds of instructions do I need to make?

While naming guardians to care for your loved one is a good start, it is important that you also leave clear and detailed written instructions concerning the type of care you want provided. Otherwise, you risk leaving the guardians in the dark about the responsibilities being entrusted to them. You are the most knowledgeable concerning your loved one's needs and are in the best position to provide these instructions. Needed instructions include the following:

- A summary of your loved one's medical history, medications, physicians, and daily care needs;

- A review of your loved one's daily routine, habits, and likes and dislikes;

- A list of your loved one's friends and their contact in formation;

- A list of your loved one's favorite hobbies, recreation, clubs, spiritual care givers, and other organizations that provide assistance;

- A statement of your desires regarding the living arrange ments to be provided for your loved one;

- A statement of the benefits and services (both government and nonprofit) that your loved one is re ceiving or may be eligible to receive in the future; and

- An explanation of your hopes and dreams for your loved one's future.

By including these detailed instructions in your estate plan, the caregivers you choose will better understand and perform their responsibilities. This will help ensure your loved one continues to receive the same loving care that you have been providing. It is like the passing of a baton – the better the instructions are, the better prepared the new guardians will be when they accept the responsibilities handed over to them. Even great instructions are not enough. You also need to put a sound financial plan in place for the management of the money that will provide the financial support for your loved one.

Why do I need to put a financial plan in place?

It is necessary to put a sound financial plan in place to provide for the care of your loved one because all the great instructions in the world will mean little if your caregivers do not have the money to carry them out. Our clients want their loved ones to receive more than the bare minimum level of care that the government provides. They want their loved ones to have the best life possible given their special needs.

Do you want to provide your loved one better than basic housing and living arrangements? Do you want your loved one to receive better medical and dental care than the government supplies? Do you want your loved one to have access to vocational training and other educational opportunities? Do you want your loved one to have access to transportation, furnishings, clothing, and other things needed to make life as normal as possible? If so, then you need to financially prepare for these things. It takes an experienced estate planning attorney and a qualified financial planner working together to establish and maintain a financial plan to ensure that your loved one will have the needed resources.

What is the role of the financial planner?

It is up to you to determine what government benefits are available for your loved one. A good financial planner will be able to calculate the cost of providing your loved one the lifestyle that you want him or her to receive beyond that which the government is willing to pay. Once these amounts are determined, the financial planner will recommend various ways to ensure there are sufficient resources to meet the shortfall between the lifestyle the government will pay for and the lifestyle you desire for your loved one.

An important part of this analysis is to make sure enough assets are available throughout your loved one's life. Your financial advisor can help you explore your options and ensure enough financial resources exist to meet your planning goals. Depending on the circumstances, your financial advisor may recommend life insurance, annuities, bonds, mutual funds, or other investments. Regardless of the specific investments selected, it is critical that your financial plan be coordinated with your estate plan. Failure to do so can cause the loss of all government benefits. To avoid this tragedy, make sure that you work with an estate planning attorney who has special needs planning experience.

How can an estate planning attorney help prevent the loss of government benefits?

A good financial plan must be designed so your loved one will not be disqualified from receiving government benefits. An experienced estate planning attorney knows how to avoid the legal pitfalls that can threaten the financial legacy you leave your child or adult with special needs.

Nothing could be worse than having the government declare that the inheritance you left your loved one makes him or her ineligible for benefits. If this happens, the government will deny or cancel the aid it would have otherwise provided for your loved one. Even worse, it could force your loved one to undergo the difficult process of reapplying for government benefits once the inheritance is depleted. This is a planning disaster that must be avoided!

How can I leave my loved one an inheritance that will not result in a disqualification of benefits?

Fortunately, a very special kind of trust can be used to leave an inheritance that will not disqualify a loved one with special needs from receiving government benefits. These are known as "Special Needs Trusts." They are designed so that assets in the trust will supplement—but not replace—the government benefits. Since the assets are held in trust, they do not legally belong to your loved one (even though the trust assets must be used solely to enhance your loved one's life). The government will not count the inherited trust assets against your loved one and jeopardize his or her eligibility for benefits.

Why bother with a trust when I can just give money to someone and tell them to use it for my loved one's care?

Giving money directly to someone else to care for your loved one (even to a trusted child or friend), instead of leaving the inheritance in a Special Needs Trust, has many hidden risks. These risks exist because when you give your assets to someone, they become the legal owner of them. This can have unfortunate consequences such as:

- If that person becomes disabled, the law requires that the assets be spent on his or her care instead of on your loved one's care;

- If that person dies, the law requires that the assets be distributed according to that person's estate plan;

- If that person has financial difficulties, the assets might be lost to that person's creditors;

- If that person goes through a divorce, the assets might be lost to an ex-spouse; and

- If that person wants to, he can spend the assets how ever he wants (and not necessarily for your child's care) since legally the assets belong to him.

For all of these reasons, and many others, protecting assets in a Special Needs Trust is much wiser than leaving them at risk as described above.

What are some other reasons to leave assets in a Special Needs Trust?

As mentioned earlier, if you do not implement an estate plan that protects your child with special needs, a judge will impose a plan of his own choosing on the family. To determine whether the judge's plan is likely to be the one you would choose for your loved one, just ask yourself a few questions:

- Will the judge appoint the trustee I would want to manage the assets I leave my loved one? *Francina In charge*

- Will the judge's plan keep my child's financial and legal affairs private instead of making them a public record?

- Will the judge's plan require that the assets I leave my loved one be distributed to my loved one for only the purposes I want, when I want, and how I want?

- Will the judge's plan result in the least costs and delays to my family?

You simply cannot ensure that the decisions of some unknown judge sitting in some unknown courtroom at some unknown time in the future will decide things the same way you would. The truth of the matter is that the decisions of many judges would be exactly opposite of how you would conduct your own private affairs.

Unless you designate who will protect your child's assets, a judge will choose for you. The judge, due to open record laws, may allow anyone to rifle through the court file and learn the size and extent of your child's assets. There is no guarantee that the judge's plan will provide the same lifestyle that you desire for your loved one. It can take years for cases to go through the stressful, expensive, and time-consuming court bureaucracy.

If the above listing of the risks of leaving things in the hands of a judge were not bad enough, any plan created by a judge will be subject to the judge's "continuing jurisdiction" over the administration of your loved one's assets. This means that the person appointed by the judge to administer your child's assets must file financial reports with the judge every year for as long as your loved one lives. This not only imposes additional annual costs of administering the judge's plan (at your loved one's expense), but it places one more intrusive and disruptive burden on your loved one.

The judge's plan will also disqualify your loved one from receiving government benefits if your loved one is deemed to personally own the assets. A well-crafted Special Needs Trust written according to your instructions will protect the confidentiality of your loved one's private affairs and preserve your loved one's right to receive government benefits.

As seen, there are many challenges involved with planning for a loved one with special needs, but they are not insurmountable. With experienced counseling and good planning they can be overcome. If you want the peace of mind that comes from knowing you have done everything possible to protect your loved one, then a Special Needs Trust needs to be part of your comprehensive estate plan.

CHAPTER FIVE

ESTATE PLANNING FOR SECOND MARRIAGES

In most "first marriages" estate plans, the couple plans for the surviving spouse to have access to all of the assets at the death of the first spouse. Typically, the couple also wants the assets split equally among their children at the death of the surviving spouse, but such planning seldom meets the needs of "second marriage" families. A second marriage creates unique circumstances that require special planning.

What circumstances are unique to second marriages?

Here are just some of the special planning circumstances that confront many couples in a second marriage:

- One spouse wants to keep property in his or her own name.

- One spouse does not want to be responsible for the other's debts.

- Each has differing investment philosophies.

- They desire different beneficiaries for their life insurance policies, annuities, and retirement accounts.

- They want their estate to be distributed to different beneficiaries (such as their respective children from their previous marriages, siblings, parents, or charities).

- The difference in age between the children from the previous marriages and the children of the new marriage requires special planning for guardianships, college expenses, and the ultimate distribution of the inheritance.

While these situations are common to most second marriages, every family is different and will have unique challenges that require special planning.

How do I plan for these challenges?

You and your future spouse should sign a prenuptial agreement that protects your rights to your property and clarifies your obligations to each other. The best time to plan for these challenges is before the wedding.

Do I really need a prenuptial agreement?

Yes. Although many couples might find it rather unromantic to discuss signing a prenuptial agreement, if either of you has been divorced, then you already know how important a prenuptial agreement can be. In the event the marriage does not work out, your prenuptial agreement may prevent you from losing your own property. The agreement will also give you the peace of mind of being able to create your own personal estate plan that leaves your property to the beneficiaries of your choice. A well-thought-out agreement will avoid misunderstandings and prevent problems from developing later.

Unfortunately, many couples avoid discussing a prenuptial agreement because they do not want to appear distrustful. A better approach is to go into a new marriage with a clear understanding of what belongs to each spouse and what will be jointly owned. For all these reasons, it is a good idea to have a well-drafted agreement in place before your wedding.

Will my prenuptial agreement survive a legal challenge?

A great deal of thought and skill is required to draft a prenuptial agreement if it is to survive a legal challenge. If you want it to work, an attorney with the requisite expertise should prepare the agreement. This is definitely not the time to get a form off the Internet and attempt to do it yourself. It must be rock solid if you want it to survive a court challenge, because a judge might rule that your entire prenuptial agreement is invalid if it fails to follow the letter of the law. The last thing you want is to have your prenuptial agreement thrown out of court because it did not meet all the technical legal requirements!

Is it too late if we are already married?

Fortunately, it is not too late to do second marriage planning even after your wedding. As long as you and your spouse are in agreement, you can still plan the division of your property by jointly signing a postnuptial agreement. A postnuptial agreement is the same as a prenuptial agreement, but it is signed after you are married. It is not unusual that couples find it much more difficult to agree on property and estate planning issues after they say their vows. Once the glow of the honeymoon has faded, the sense of urgency is lost. To ensure you are able to reach an agreement, planning with a prenuptial agreement is preferable.

Do I still need an estate plan if I have a prenuptial or postnuptial agreement in place?

Absolutely! Your prenuptial or postnuptial agreement merely gives you and your new spouse the right to separately control and plan for the distribution of your respective estates. You must still do the planning if you want to stay in control of your estate and have it distributed after your death according to your desires.

What type of planning do I need to do?

The type of planning that you need to do depends on the goals that you want to accomplish. Joint tenancy ownership, payable on death designations (PODs), beneficiary designations, trusts, and wills are important tools that you can use to plan your estate. Whether or not any of these tools are right for you can be determined only after a careful analysis of all of your assets along with a thoughtful review of what you want done with each individual asset. Great caution is necessary because the improper use of any estate planning strategy can backfire and result in the disinheritance of your intended beneficiaries.

For example, when entering a second marriage many couples want to satisfy the dual goals of protecting their new spouse while also leaving an inheritance for the children of their previous marriages. To accomplish this goal, they each sign new "I love you wills." These wills are often drafted to state that upon the death of either spouse, all of their assets will be distributed first to the surviving spouse and then, when the second dies, to the children of the previous marriages. Although the couple thinks they have done a good job of planning their estates with wills, they have not! Planning with wills, without taking other precautions, is a big mistake for several reasons.

First, unless all of the assets of each spouse are carefully analyzed, it is entirely possible that the surviving spouse will receive nothing from the "I love you will." This is because the will may fail to control the distribution of any property in an individual's estate. Instead, the entire estate may be distributed via beneficiary designations on life insurance policies and retirement accounts; payable on death (POD) or joint tenancy designations on savings and checking accounts; and joint tenancy designations on real estate, all of which override the will. If the first spouse to die failed to get around to removing the children of the previous marriage as the ones to receive all of his or her property through these types of transfers, the surviving spouse of the new marriage gets nothing because the will was meaningless!

A second planning mistake is much like the first, only this time it is the children who are disinherited. People who remarry usually want to protect their new spouse and still leave an inheritance to the children of the first marriage. The second marriage couple dutifully goes to their attorney to sign new wills. They are often drafted to leave half of the estate to the new spouse and the other half to the children of the previous marriage. Although they leave the attorney's office feeling proud and thinking that all of their loved ones are now protected, they are mistaken.

Consider this scenario: The first parent dies and the children are dismayed to learn that in the intervening years, the parent's house, car, bank accounts, and investment accounts were all titled jointly with the stepparent. They further learn that the stepparent was named as the beneficiary of their parent's IRA and life insurance policy. Even though the will left one-half of the property to them, the children are effectively disinherited because of the improper use of joint tenancy and beneficiary designations. The stepparent gets it all – the children get nothing.

This was the estate plan of Cinderella's father! Although Cinderella should have inherited at least part of her father's estate, everything, including the home, went to her stepmother. Good estate planning can avoid this type of tragedy.

A third planning mistake occurs when a couple writes their wills to state that on the first spouse's death everything goes to the survivor and that on the second death everything is to be divided between the children of both spouses. The fault in this plan is that it assumes that there will be assets left to pass on after the second spouse's death. In reality, there might be nothing left to pass if the assets are all consumed by the surviving spouse due to medical expenses, nursing home costs, or other unforeseen circumstances. Even if there are assets left over, with "I love you wills" there is nothing to prevent the surviving spouse from rewriting his or her will after the first spouse dies and disinheriting the stepchildren.

Good estate planning is needed to protect not only the inheritance you leave your spouse, but also the inheritance you want to ultimately leave to your children. An experienced estate planning attorney will draft what is needed to make sure that none of your loved ones suffer these planning disasters.

How can I prevent these types of planning disasters?

We believe that the cornerstone of a good estate plan is a revocable living trust. A trust can help avoid the planning mistakes we have discussed. With a revocable living trust, one set of instructions will exist to control the distribution of all of your property. This is because the trust can be – when done correctly – both the owner of all of your property while you are alive (including your home, checking account, and investment accounts) and the beneficiary of your life insurance and retirement accounts. Since your trust will be both the owner andor beneficiary of all of your property, you can be confident that all of your property will be distributed the way you want to those you want.

Planning with a revocable living trust will give you the peace of mind of knowing that your desires will not be disrupted by the haphazard use of property titles and beneficiary designations that could otherwise leave your property to unintended heirs. Since all of your assets will be controlled by the instructions in your trust, your planning goals will be fully met. Your spouse and children will actually receive the portion of your estate that you want them to have. These and other protections are important when planning in a second marriage to protect both your new spouse and the children of your first marriage.

What other protections do I need to consider in a second marriage?

There is no "one size fits all" set of estate planning protections that is appropriate for all people at all times. You are unique, your loved ones are unique, the assets you own are unique, and the goals you have for how you want to protect your loved ones and property are unique. The combination of all of these factors is why, if you are entering a second marriage, it is important to assemble your estate planning team of professionals (estate planning attorney, accountant, financial planner, and insurance professional) and discuss your goals with the team. This allows them to analyze your situation and advise you concerning the particular provisions you need to have in place for your personal situation. You should be prepared to review, discuss, and receive their counsel concerning the following:

- The assets owned by both you and your spouse;

- Your respective investment philosophies;

- A careful review of each spouse's beneficiary designations to make sure that outdated decisions will not cause unintended consequences;

- The goals you and your new spouse are trying to accomplish for yourselves, for your children from previous marriages, and for any children of the new marriage;

- The advisability of having a prenuptial or postnuptial agreement to classify your property;

- The importance of having new heath care and financial powers of attorney to appoint appropriate individuals to carry out your directions;

- An analysis of retirement plans and Social Security benefits to maximize available income for the two of you during your joint lifetimes and to provide for the surviving spouse; and

- How Family Trusts and QTIP (Qualified Terminable Interest Property) Trusts can ensure the needs of the surviving spouse are met while also meeting the needs of the children.

What are Family Trusts and QTIP Planning?

Special planning is required when a second marriage couple desires to protect the inheritance of both the surviving spouse and the children. Without this special planning, the danger exists that one or the other can become disinherited. Family Trusts and QTIP planning prevent this tragedy.

Here is how they work:

The estate plans of many second marriage couples are designed so that the estate of the first spouse to die is divided into two separate trusts. The first trust is referred to as the "Family Trust" since it is usually designed to benefit the entire family (spouse and children). This trust takes advantage of the deceased spouse's estate tax "applicable exclusion" (an amount that the deceased spouse can leave to the beneficiaries' tax-free).

The instructions of your Family Trust can state that the estate's tax-free assets are to be used to benefit your surviving spouse, along with any children you wish to benefit, in exactly the manner that you want them benefited. During the lifetime of the surviving spouse, the income and principal of the Family Trust can be distributed based upon the needs of both the surviving spouse and the children. This means that you can guarantee that both receive an inheritance!

If your estate has more assets than can be placed in the Family Trust tax-free, the excess assets are then "spilled" into a second trust that is designed to benefit only the surviving spouse for the surviving spouse's lifetime. This second trust is called a Qualified Terminable Interest Property (QTIP) trust because the surviving spouse has only a "qualified" lifetime right to the trust's assets that "terminates" at the spouse's death. The remainder of the QTIP trust can then be distributed as you direct. Under the special rules for the QTIP trust, your surviving spouse is entitled to all of the income of the trust, which must be distributed at least annually. You also have the discretion to give your spouse access to the principal of the trust if you choose to do so.

Property placed in a QTIP trust qualifies for an estate tax marital deduction. This means that the trust's assets are subject to estate taxation only after the death of the surviving spouse. Thus your spouse can obtain the full tax-free benefits of the trust's assets during his or her lifetime.

Although the lifetime estate tax-free benefits of the Family and QTIP Ttrusts for a surviving spouse and children are considerable, this is not its most important feature. The most important feature takes place when the surviving spouse dies. It is then that any remaining assets of the trust must be distributed according to your instructions (not according to the desires of your spouse who might be tempted to leave it to a new spouse or to the children of the new spouse). This type of planning affords you the confidence of knowing that any remaining assets in the Family or QTIP Ttrusts will go to your children or other beneficiaries exactly as you want.

Although Family and QTIP Ttrusts offer many attractive planning opportunities in first or subsequent marriages, like all other estate planning tools, they should be considered in light of the specific planning desires of each family. It is a strategy that should only be used after a detailed discussion of your planning goals with the estate planning attorney concerning how to best protect all of your loved ones.

CHAPTER SIX

ESTATE PLANNING FOR SINGLES AND UNMARRIED COUPLES

If estate planning is important for married couples, it is even more important for those who are single—including unmarried couples. This is because the law affords fewer legal protections to those who are single (whether living alone or with a partner) than it does to married couples. This lack of legal rights can have serious consequences if you fail to plan.

What serious consequences will I face if, being a single person, I do not plan my estate?

Married couples face a host of issues when they fail to plan their estates. As a single person, you face the same difficulties—and many more. Here are some of the most common problems unique to singles:

- Singles have special problems with state intestacy laws. When one spouse of a marriage dies without an estate plan, state law protects the surviving spouse by guaranteeing that he or she receives some or all of the decedent's property. Single people have no such inheritance rights, which means that their loved ones are often disinherited. This is because state inheritance laws dictate who receives the deceased's property based solely on how closely one is related by blood. The law leaves nothing to those related to the deceased by friendship or love—no matter how committed or long-term the relationship. The consequence is that, without a proper estate plan, the entire estate can go to unintended heirs, including distant or estranged relatives. Even unmarried persons who have been living together for decades have no protection. The law treats them like strangers if one of them dies without a valid trust or will naming the other as a beneficiary.

- Singles are not protected by pension laws. Only spouses are protected under the Employee Retirement Income Security Act (ERISA). Even those with a lifetime relationship to the deceased receive nothing of his or her pension unless special planning is done. Some states are starting to recognize the rights of domestic partners, but these rights are extremely limited.

- Singles cannot roll inherited IRAs into their own IRAs. This right is available only to a surviving spouse. In order for the surviving loved ones of a single person to defer withdrawals from the deceased's IRA, and continue to have it grow tax deferred, special elections must be made.

- Singles do not have the legal ability to make unlimited tax-free transfers of property to others. Only married couples have the legal right to transfer property between themselves without triggering gift and estate tax consequences—an important strategy in avoiding estate taxes. This means that the entire estate of a deceased spouse can be transferred gift and estate tax free to the surviving spouse so that every penny is available to support the survivor for the rest of his or her life. Unfortunately, the beneficiaries of a single person will receive their share only after it has been subjected to taxes. The sad consequence is that a single person's estate is often required to immediately pay taxes leaving less money available to support a surviving partner or other loved ones.

- Singles who are not the biological or adoptive parent of minor children do not automatically qualify as guardian of their partner's children. When singles fail to nominate the guardian they want for their children, court battles inevitably erupt over who will gain custody of the children.

- Singles are excluded from the special legal rights given to married couples in community property states. These states presume equal ownership of all assets and provide spouses with statutory protections from being disinherited. Singles have none of these rights.

- Singles have special concerns regarding health care decisions. It is exceptionally important that singles have the proper health care documents in place to authorize the people they trust the most to carry out their wishes. If a single person fails to sign the proper health care documents, estranged family members (or even strangers) might be appointed by the courts to make those decisions. Trusted friends, or even cohabitating partners, have no legal standing to go to court and be named as health care agents for each other. Without proper planning, a domestic partner may even be prohibited from visiting his or her loved one in the hospital due to new federal privacy legislation (HIPAA).

Singles face many unique and serious challenges that can have grave consequences for you and your loved ones—if you fail to plan. These include, among others, inheritance laws that ignore relationships among unmarried adults; tax pitfalls involving pensions, IRAs, gifts, and property transfers during lifetime and at death; guardianship for your minor children; property rights; or the court appointment of undesired guardians to oversee your care. Because of these special planning needs, you must act to protect yourself and your loved ones. You should not be fooled into believing that, just because you are single, your needs are simple and can be solved without any planning or by merely using joint tenancy and beneficiary designations.

Why shouldn't I use joint tenancy and beneficiary designations to transfer my assets?

Instead of using good estate planning techniques, many singles simply pass their assets to each other by transferring everything into joint tenancy and designating each other as the surviving beneficiary. This is not advised. While you can use joint tenancy and beneficiary designations to avoid the probating of your assets following your death, you still face the same pitfalls that married couples face when they transfer assets in this manner. Many problems exist with joint tenancy ownership. One major pitfall is that joint tenancy designations merely postpone probate court proceedings until the death of the surviving joint tenant; they do not eliminate probate. Another concern is that creditors can claim the joint tenancy property of either joint owner. This means that your joint tenant's creditor woes can jeopardize your share of the property. The joint tenant who dies first loses control over who receives the property when the survivor dies. If you are the first to pass, the surviving joint tenant can leave the property to anyone, including someone you detest!

How can I avoid these pitfalls?

If you are single and want to avoid the pitfalls discussed above, you are advised to make sure that your estate plan contains at least three critical documents: A carefully drafted revocable living trust, a durable power of attorney, and a power of attorney for health care. The instructions in your revocable living trust will keep you in control of your property throughout your life, provide instructions concerning how your property is to be protected if you become incapacitated, and enable you to leave your property to whom you want, how you want, and when you want. Your durable power of attorney will provide legal authority to those you want to handle legal issues on your behalf if you are incapacitated. Your power of attorney for health care will make sure that only those you trust will be authorized to make health care decisions for you, and only according to the instructions you provide.

If you are a single person and cannot take advantage of the unlimited marital deduction that married couples use to bypass gift and estate taxes, your estate plan must be drafted very carefully to take full advantage of every opportunity to avoid these taxes. Otherwise, your loved ones may be forced to pay unnecessary gift or death taxes.

Many people are unaware that the death proceeds of life insurance are subject to estate tax. One way that you can eliminate these taxes for your loved ones is to use an irrevocable life insurance trust in addition to your revocable trust. Life insurance held in an irrevocable life insurance trust is exempt from estate taxes. This arrangement will not only ensure that your loved ones are provided with the assets (life insurance death benefits) needed to take care of them after you pass on, it will do so tax free. Other planning strategies are available to lessen the tax burden on your loved ones. If you are single, it is especially important to consult an experienced estate planning attorney who will be able to advise you on both the tax-related and non-tax-related reasons for you to plan your estate.

What are some non-tax-related reasons for singles to plan their estates?

There are many non-tax reasons for singles to create a solid estate plan. First and foremost, you probably want to maintain control of your assets throughout your entire life. By giving specific instructions as to how your property is to be used to take care of your loved ones, you maintain control of your estate while you are alive, in the event of incapacity, and even after death.

Another important planning issue for singles concerns property distributions. While married couples with children usually want their assets to flow first to their surviving spouse and then to their children, singles often have different desires. Even partners in committed relationships can have different wishes concerning the distribution of their respective property. By using trusts, each person can name the other as a lifetime beneficiary and still have the ability to designate different ultimate beneficiaries. For example, one unmarried partner may want his estate to go to his parents, while the other partner may want her estate to go to siblings, other loved ones, or to charity. Each person gets to decide what is best.

Many singles additionally take advantage of business law to supplement their estate plans. By establishing business entities, such as corporations and limited liability companies, singles can formulate a business plan and designate how business assets are to be distributed following incapacity or death.

As a single person, you cannot take advantage of the laws that benefit only married couples. Nonetheless, you can still address the unique planning challenges that you face through the use of living trusts, durable powers of attorney, health care powers, irrevocable trusts, business entities, and other estate planning strategies. It is wise to take advantage of these tools to help you achieve your desired planning goals.

CHAPTER SEVEN

INSURANCE AND LONG TERM CARE

The statistics are startling: If you live past age sixty-five, you have a 50 percent chance of needing nursing home care at some point in your life. Your chances increase to 60 percent if you live past age seventy-five. The likelihood that you will need such care makes it even more important to plan for your health care needs now! The first step is to examine your long-term care options.

What are my long-term care options?

If you find yourself needing long-term care, the most common options include:

• Receiving care in your own home;

• Receiving care in someone else's home;

- Receiving care in an assisted living facility; or

- Receiving care in a nursing home.

Each of these care options has its own advantages and disadvantages.

Receiving care in your own home is a wonderful option, ~~but~~ *and* it is the choice our clients overwhelmingly state that they prefer. You get to interview and personally select your own health care providers instead of relying on the employees hired by an assisted living facility or nursing home. You get to stay in the familiar and comfortable surroundings of your own home with ready access to your possessions. It is also where your personal privacy and security is best protected.

The disadvantage of home care is that it is very expensive. This option is typically available only for people who have the substantial financial resources needed to pay for it out of their own pockets or have long-term care insurance in place. If you need round-the-clock assistance, care in your own home will likely cost almost twice as much as care at a nursing home. In addition, most homes are not designed for in-home care. You may have problems with steps, doors, width of hallways, and kitchen and bathroom accessibility that necessitate costly modifications to your home.

Your second care option is to be cared for in someone else's home. If you have this option, you are most fortunate. If a family member is providing care, your costs will be greatly reduced, and you will have the benefit of being surrounded by people who love you and will monitor your care.

Receiving care in someone else's home also has its disadvantages. You may be required to move away from your friends and familiar surroundings. Your health needs may also place a significant financial and emotional burden on your new caregivers. For instance, they may have to undergo expensive modifications to their home in order to accommodate your care.

Your third option, and the one growing at the fastest rate, is to receive care at an assisted living facility. A major benefit of this option is that you retain the privacy of having your own apartment or room. You will also be relieved of the burden of preparing your own meals; food will be provided for you in a community dining room. The level of care available to you can vary from basic services that promote independent living to more comprehensive services that can provide assistance with bathing, dressing, or toileting. Of course, this means you will be living outside the comfort and privacy of your own home, your care providers will be the employees of the facility instead of being personally selected by you, and the expense of the care will be paid for out of your own pocket.

Nursing homes are usually the care option of last resort. One advantage is that they provide the highest level of care for those who need it the most. The beds at nursing homes are usually reserved for those who have profound physical disabilities or those who suffer mental disabilities such as dementia and Alzheimer's disease. Because of the efficiencies of providing care to a number of individuals in one facility, the cost of nursing home care is less than you would expect to pay if you received help from personal care providers in your own residence.

On the downside, nursing homes provide their residents the least privacy and usually the least comfortable surroundings of all the options. Instead of a private apartment, most residents live in a shared, sterile environment that is one step away from that of a hospital. The keepsake personal effects of nursing home residents are often limited to what can fit on the top of a nightstand.

Despite the shortcomings of nursing homes, such facilities are the only option for those who require assistance but are unable to pay for it themselves. Even if you could be adequately cared for in an assisted living facility (which costs about half of nursing home care, offers better privacy and provides a more comfortable environment), you might still be forced into a nursing home because only nursing homes are eligible to receive the government benefits needed to pay for the long-term care of disabled individuals. Therefore, if you prefer a long-term care option other than nursing home care, you are strongly advised to plan now so you have the resources to pay for the type of care you desire later.

Are there other reasons why I should plan for long-term care?

It is important to understand that all long-term care costs *this* must be self-paid until you exhaust your own financial resources. Only when you are indigent are you eligible to receive government assistance. *Broke*

Here is another hard reality: Within just a few short years, hundreds of thousands of dollars will be required to pay for the long-term care needs of a disabled individual. If you self-pay for your own care, or the care needs of a disabled spouse, these costs can devastate your life savings and cripple your lifestyle. Few families have the resources necessary to withstand this type of a financial hit. Consequently, it is a good idea to determine your best option to pay for the potential cost of long-term care well in advance. Planning ahead will give you the peace of mind of knowing that resources exist to provide the care you desire without destroying your financial security.

What is my best option to prepare for long-term care costs?

If you want to ensure that you have the resources needed to pay for your future long-term care needs, your best option is to purchase a long-term care insurance policy. You should not wait to investigate the coverage that is available. The biggest mistake you can make with long-term care insurance is to wait until you are too old or too ill to qualify for it or can no longer afford to pay the insurance premiums. Be aware that long-term care insurance coverage gets increasingly expensive as you age. The sooner you get it, the lower your annual cost.

What is long-term care insurance?

Long-term care insurance is a special type of insurance policy that is designed to pay some or all of your long-term care needs if you become disabled. Although this insurance is commonly referred to as "nursing home insurance," many policies contain options that also pay for "in-home" care or for assisted living. If you become disabled, having this option will enable you to avoid the more restrictive nursing home environment for as long as possible.

Even if your care needs exceed what can be provided at home or in an assisted living facility, your long-term care policy will provide you the financial resources needed to choose the care facility you prefer. This is important because many nursing homes will not accept patients who depend upon government assistance (Medicaid) to pay for their care. Your insurance will give you the preferred status of being a private pay patient, which increases your chances of receiving the care you need at the facility you want.

If you wish to avoid the devastating impact long-term care costs may have on your estate, we strongly suggest that you ask your estate planning attorney to recommend a qualified long-term care insurance professional. These specialists help you navigate the differences that exist between the policies issued by various providers so that you can choose the best option for you and your loved ones.

What kind of differences exist between long-term care policies?

There are many differences between policies. Insurance companies vary greatly in the benefits they offer and the premiums they charge. Without guidance from an insurance specialist, the choices can be overwhelming. Here are some important factors to consider when purchasing long-term care insurance:

- The coverage period (the number of years of care the policy pays);

- The maximum dollar amount the company will pay for each day of care;

- Whether the policy will pay for in-home care or assisted living;

- Whether the policy provides a premium refund for unused insurance;

- The elimination period (the number of days that a disability exists before coverage starts);

- Whether payment for care can be made to a family member or only to licensed professionals;

- Whether the policy provides for inflation protection; and

- The financial soundness of the insurance company (you want to choose a company that is likely to still be in business when you need them).

The large number of options makes it difficult to discuss long-term care insurance policies in general terms. Like other estate planning issues, long-term care insurance must be tailored to your particular needs. Keep this in mind when talking to friends, relatives, and neighbors. What works for your brother-in-law may not work for you. What is prohibitively expensive for your neighbor may be entirely affordable for you. The only way to know what is right for you and what your policy covers is to review your options with your estate planning team of professionals. Your estate planning attorney and long-term care insurance specialist will design a plan specifically for your needs, goals, and budget.

Typically, the cost of staying in a nursing home for only a few months will be greater than the lifetime cost of the long-term care insurance premium! When you consider the various risks that you are insuring against, the cost of such insurance is a real bargain.

Can I still qualify for long-term care insurance if I have existing health problems?

Do not make the common mistake of assuming that you cannot get long-term care insurance just because you have a pre-existing condition. The long-term care insurance industry is constantly developing and evolving. While it is true that some companies may refuse coverage because of a certain medical condition, other companies may completely ignore it. You must consult with a long-term care insurance specialist to know what your options are before you can make a truly educated decision.

The bottom line: You and your family could suffer a catastrophic financial loss if you require long-term care. Your best protection against this type of disaster is to obtain a properly designed long-term care insurance policy from an insurance specialist. Such insurance should be an integral part of your comprehensive estate plan.

CHAPTER EIGHT

MEDICAID PLANNING

There are three basic ways to pay for nursing home and other long-term care: pay for it yourself, insure for it, or rely on government aid. This chapter discusses the "government aid" option, which is known as Medicaid.

What is Medicaid?

Medicaid is a government funded, needs- based program designed to pay for nursing home care and other long-term care for those who cannot afford it themselves. Until recently, Medicaid was only available for long-term care in a skilled nursing facility. Many states have now adopted (or are adopting) laws that extend Medicaid coverage to care at home, in assisted living facilities, or in other residential care options beyond nursing homes. To qualify for Medicaid, you must be "indigent," which means that you have limited income, almost no savings, and only those assets that the government permits (known as "exempt" assets). In addition, you must be functionally impaired so as to need significant help with your daily living needs.

Although Medicaid is a federal program, Medicaid benefits are administered by the states. The law gives each state some latitude in determining whether an individual is indigent and eligible for Medicaid benefits. To determine if an individual is indigent, the state will examine whether the individual meets the state's income and asset tests. There are different tests depending upon whether the person applying for benefits is single or married. Medicaid benefits are also only available for U.S. citizens and qualified aliens. Also, it is important not to confuse the benefits provided by Medicaid with the benefits provided by a different federal program, Medicare.

What is Medicare and will it pay my long term care costs?

Medicare is a federal health insurance program for individuals over the age of 65 or for those who are disabled. Medicare pays only for rehabilitative care; it does not pay for "custodial" nursing home care.

To qualify for Medicare coverage, your nursing home stay must be preceded by a hospital stay of at least three days. Medicare will pay 100% of the cost for your first 20 days of nursing home care when receiving physical therapy or other rehabilitative treatment. Medicare will then pay only a portion of the next 80 days of your nursing home care. After 100 days, all Medicare benefits stop. Medicare benefits will also stop before the 100-day period elapses if you are not making any progress toward your rehabilitation and recovery. Medicare is not designed to pay for long-term custodial care, and it will not provide coverage beyond these limits.

What about my health insurance or my Medigap policy?

Like Medicare, your health insurance pays only for treatment and rehabilitative care. It will not pay for custodial care in a nursing home. Your Medigap policy is considered a supplement to Medicare benefits: it pays only if Medicare pays. These insurance policies are also known as Medicare Supplements. When you do not qualify for Medicare, or when your Medicare stops paying benefits, your Medigap policy also stops paying. Only Medicaid pays for long-term care costs.

How do I qualify for Medicaid?

To qualify for Medicaid, you must pass two economic tests. The first is an income test. If you enter a nursing home and apply for Medicaid, you are required to contribute all of your income to the cost of care, except for a small amount that you are permitted to keep for personal needs. Medicaid then pays the balance. If your income is greater than the cost of your care, you pay everything. Medicaid pays nothing.

If you are not in a nursing home, income eligibility rules are much more complicated. You will need a lawyer with expertise in this technical area of law to guide you through this minefield.

If you have a spouse living at home (known as the "community spouse" or "in-home spouse"), the income test is handled differently. The spouse at home is allowed to keep all of his or her own income and is not required to contribute to the cost of care. If your spouse has little or no income, a special rule applies that allows your spouse to keep some of your income to pay for your spouse's living expenses.

The second economic test relates to your assets. The government will screen your assets to determine if they are "exempt" or "non-exempt". Owning an exempt asset will not disqualify you from receiving Medicaid, but owning more than the permitted amount of non-exempt assets will disqualify you. The rules concerning exempt assets are different depending upon whether or not you are married.

Which assets are considered exempt assets?

The following assets are considered exempt:

- Your home;

- Your car;

- Your personal belongings; and

- A small number of other types of assets.

While laws vary from state to state, generally your personal residence is an exempt asset for purposes of Medicaid eligibility.

However, technical rules exist pertaining to how much of your home's value is exempt. In order to keep your home classified as exempt, it is advisable to express your intent to return to your home after the nursing home stay.

If you are single, your state may be permitted to place a lien on your home (under certain situations) that will be enforced when the house is sold. Although there are legal ways to require the state to release its lien, or at the least to minimize it, a thorough knowledge of the Medicaid rules is essential.

One car is exempt. Any additional vehicles will be treated as non-exempt.

In determining your Medicaid eligibility, most states typically ignore personal belongings. The exception is if your personal belongings have an unusually high value. So unless you have an original Picasso hanging on the wall, or some other valuable artwork or collection, your personal belongings are probably safe.

A small number of other assets are also not subject to the spend down requirements. These include prepaid burial plans and a small amount of life insurance. Funeral or burial assets may be of different types. Some types are subject to limitations.

What other assets can I keep?

In order to qualify for Medicaid, you cannot currently own non-exempt assets that exceed $2000.00. This applies to you as a Medicaid applicant regardless of whether you are married or single.

How much additional property is my spouse allowed to keep?

The Medicaid rules of every state provides that your in-home spouse is entitled to all of the exempt assets and an additional amount of non-exempt property. The non-exempt property includes one-half of the assets that the two of you had on the date used by Medicaid to determine your eligibility, subject to strict limitations as to the maximum amount. A community spouse with property in excess of the limit of non-exempt assets will cause your application to be denied.

Since the law allows singles and married couples to own a modest amount of assets and still qualify for Medicaid, why not try to maximize that which the government says you get to keep? So if you find yourself in the unfortunate position where you or your spouse need to apply for Medicaid, you have every right to "spend down" your assets in order to incur the shortest penalty period and keep as much of your property as the government allows. By carefully following the spend down rules, you can accomplish both goals!

Determining how to best comply with the spend down rules, while still protecting your property to the greatest extent legally allowed, requires exceptional knowledge, resourcefulness and creativity. If you want the best possible results, you need to speak with your estate planning attorney sooner rather than later.

How soon do I need to get legal advice?

The timing of your planning is dependent on your particular circumstances. For example, starting your spend down too early can cause serious problems. If you are married, you may convert some of your non-exempt assets to exempt property before the date that Medicaid uses to decide how much of your non-exempt assets your in-home spouse can keep.

If you are single, spending down or divesting in order to qualify for Medicaid before you enter a nursing home may seriously limit your placement choices.

What if I do not meet the economic tests?

If you do not meet the economic tests, you do not qualify for Medicaid, but do not panic. With the proper planning, those who fail the eligibility tests can still be helped.

For example, if you do not meet the asset test because you own too many non-exempt assets, the law gives you the right to "spend down" your non-exempt assets to the approved level. Once you reach the approved dollar amount (currently $2,000), you will qualify for Medicaid.

Spending down your assets may not be as bad as it sounds. The spend down process can involve turning your non-exempt assets (which you do not get to keep) into exempt assets (which you do get to keep). You turn one into the other. If all of your non-exempt property is converted into exempt property, then none of it is counted against you when you apply for Medicaid.

What else about the divestment rules do I need to know?

Any non-exempt assets either you or your spouse gives away without receiving something of equal value in return may be classified by the state as a "divestment." Forgiving a debt or refusing money owed to your by someone else is also considered a divestment. Such uncompensated divestments will render the applicant ineligible for Medicaid for a certain period of time, known as the "penalty period." A Medicaid penalty period is imposed because the government does not want you to deliberately impoverish yourself (by giving everything to your children or others) and then applying for Medicaid. Your intent when making gifts is important. For example, smaller regular gifts for birthdays, anniversaries, or graduations may not be classified as divestments.

I thought I could make a tax-free gift each year to my children without any problems.

Many of our clients mistakenly confuse the gift tax laws with the Medicaid eligibility rules. The amount that the IRS allows you to gift tax-free each year, otherwise known as the "annual exclusion amount," has nothing to do with Medicaid eligibility. They are different rules for different purposes. Many people have learned to their great dismay that their perfectly legal tax-free gifts were treated as divestments under the Medicaid rules, which rendered them ineligible for benefits.

What is a "lookback"?

Divestments can subject you to a penalty period for Medicaid eligibility, rendering you ineligible for benefits for a set amount of time. Only gifts made during the Medicaid "lookback" period of time will count as a divestment that incurs a penalty period. The lookback period is a specific amount of time (usually years) set by your state; any gift you make during this period can be counted as a divestment. Carefully planning your divestments to minimize or eliminate the Medicaid penalty period you incur is one of the most important skills your advisors can provide.

How is the penalty period calculated?

When you meet the income and assets levels needed to be eligible for Medicaid, you must file an application to receive benefits. In addition to disclosing your income from all sources and all of your assets, you must also identify any divestments that you made during the lookback period.

Each state has a divisor that it uses to calculate the penalty period. The divisor is reset each year, and the amount of the divisor varies from state to state. The caseworker handling your application will divide the total value of all divestment made during the lookback period by the divisor to calculate the penalty period.

As an example, let us assume that you made divestments totaling $60,000 during the lookback period. Let us further assume (for easy mathematical calculation) that the daily divisor is $200. By dividing $60,000 by $200, we find that you must serve a penalty period of 300 days before you become eligible for benefits. Under current law, the penalty period does not start until you are income and asset eligible and you have applied for Medicaid.

You can see the dilemma. If the penalty period prevents you from receiving benefits for any extended length of time, most nursing homes will not accept you as a patient unless you have the means of guaranteeing self-payment. If you gave away your property, you have no means of payment. While giving away your property (divesting it) may once have seemed like a good idea at the time, it may no longer be an attractive option if the catastrophic result is to render you ineligible for the care you need. Divestment is dangerous without both careful planning and appropriate counseling.

The guy at the barbershop said his sister-in-law's mother's best-friend gave all of her assets to her kids. Should I do the same thing?

It is amazing how much legal advice is dispensed in barbershops and beauty parlors! Unfortunately, much of this advice is just plain wrong. Whenever you divest assets, great care must be taken to make sure that it does not render you ineligible for Medicaid benefits. More than any other type of estate planning, a good long-term care plan must be individually tailored to fit your family and your assets.

The key to good estate planning is to keep you in as much control of your life and your property as possible. If you give all of your property to your children, you risk losing it to your children's creditors, to their spouses should they divorce, and to anyone else who sues them. Effective long-term care planning will protect your assets by keeping you in control of them instead of putting them at risk. You should only consider divesting your assets when done as part of a carefully crafted estate plan that is developed with the assistance of a qualified attorney. A well-designed individualized plan will allow you to stay in control of your property as long as you want and transfer it to your loved ones only when you are ready.

Will the nursing home take my house?

Remember that for purposes of determining Medicaid eligibility, your house is an exempt asset. This means your home cannot be taken from you while you are alive. However, under some circumstances the state that provides Medicaid benefits may retain the right to place a lien against your home for the value of your care. This type of lien is enforced when the house is sold. Depending upon the value of the benefits you receive, your equity in the house could be lost.

We frequently hear from our clients that they want to give their home to their children but still retain the right to continue living there as long as they want. There are many risks involved with gifting your home to your children including the following:

- If you transfer (gift) your house to the kids it will be counted as a divestment. You will be taking an exempt asset (which the state does not consider when determining Medicaid eligibility), and turning it into a non-exempt asset (one that is subject to a penalty period). While some states allow Medicaid applicants to transfer a non-exempt asset without penalty, most will impose a penalty period on the transfer of the house.

- Your home will now be at risk from the claims of your children's creditors. Your children's creditors, divorcing spouses, business debts, and lawsuits can present a bigger danger than the state's lien.

- Your children may incur capital gains taxes when the house is sold that could have been avoided had they inherited the property from you after your death.

These and other problems can strike those who gift their property away without careful planning.

What other problems could happen if I give my property to my kids?

Everyone assumes that their children will outlive them. But what happens if one of your children dies first? Your property will likely be tied up in probate court and distributed according to that child's Will. If your child does not have a Will, state law will control the distribution. In either case this may result in the wrong people getting your property. If transferring title of your house was your attempt to preserve the value for your family, your planning goal has failed.

If the gifting of your house is an important option for you to consider, it is critical that it be done correctly. If you do it at the wrong time or under the wrong circumstances, you will be creating more problems than you are solving. Rather than just giving your house away to avoid nursing home costs, a possible solution is to place it in a Medicaid Trust.

What is a Medicaid Trust?

A Medicaid Trust is a special irrevocable trust created by you during your lifetime for the purpose of holding title to your home and other assets. The Medicaid Trust can maintain your right to live in your home, as well as the right to choose the trustees. Because these trusts offer management and legal protection of the assets you place in them, they provide an excellent option for those who are concerned about protecting their estates from the impact of nursing home care costs. Nonetheless, there are important factors that must be considered to determine if it is the right choice for you

Medicaid Trusts are irrevocable. Therefore, once you create one you cannot change it. This is usually not a problem, since all of the trust's instructions are written by you to benefit only you and others of your choosing. You can also retain the right to use all of the income earned by the trust's assets. Further, by prohibiting your access to the principal in the trust, those assets (including your house) are not considered owned by you when determining your Medicaid eligibility.

However, you need to be aware that a transfer of your house or other property into your Medicaid Trust will be treated as a divestment that will trigger a penalty period. This means that it is best to create your Medicaid Trust and transfer your property into it while you are still healthy. The goal is to create and fund your trust and complete the entire lookback period well before you need to apply for Medicaid.

A Medicaid Trust can be drafted to allow you to change beneficiaries and direct the distribution of trust property to your beneficiaries at your death. More importantly, it can allow the distribution of trust property to your beneficiaries during your lifetime. Since the divestment occurred when the property went into the Medicaid Trust, distributions during the lookback period can be made to your beneficiaries without creating a penalty period. Because your property is held in trust you eliminate the concern that your property is lost because a child divorces, dies, or gets sued. The Medicaid Trust also allows your beneficiaries to receive the tax benefits of receiving property as an inheritance rather than as a gift.

To summarize, there are substantial advantages to creating and funding a Medicaid Trust. Needless to say, special knowledge and skill is needed to draft a Medicaid Trust so that it complies with both federal and state law.

Do I need a Medicaid Trust if I already have a Revocable Living Trust?

While a revocable trust is the foundation of many good estate plans, by itself your revocable trust will not protect your assets from nursing home care costs. A Medicaid Trust may be needed to obtain this additional protection.

If you are not ready now to create your own Medicaid Trust, you can still authorize the trustee of your revocable trust (or the agent of your power of attorney) to activate a nursing home plan for you when needed. This requires drafting special instructions to make sure that your plan is followed. An estate planning attorney whose practice is dedicated to helping clients explore these complex issues should be consulted to see if this option is preferable to creating a Medicaid Trust now.

CHAPTER NINE

HELPING PARENTS PLAN

If the subject of sex is taboo between you and your parents, just wait for their reaction when you ask them about the details of their estate plan! Seniors face a variety of issues unique to their stage in life (retirement, physical or mental limitations, reduced financial resources, the loss of friends, and their own mortality). Many find it difficult to even think of these issues, let alone discuss them with others—especially their children. As a result, it may be difficult for you to learn if your parents have properly planned their estate.

The consequence of this lack of communication is that you might be deprived of the information needed to ensure that your parents' estate planning wishes will be carried out. It may also deprive you of the information you need to ensure that the administration of their estate will not cause you and other surviving family members to needlessly suffer the many problems associated with unplanned (or poorly planned) estates. These can include probate and guardianship court hearings, legal contests, undue delays, loss of privacy, and taxes that good planning could have avoided.

This chapter is designed to help you effectively engage your parents in a productive conversation about estate planning. It will give you the information you need to overcome the many challenges that prevent seniors from having a good estate plan in place and show you how to spot the red flags that warrant an immediate discussion with your parents regarding the planning they have or have not done.

What are the red flags that indicate I need to talk with my parents?

The following family scenarios prompt an immediate need to broach the topic of estate planning:

- Your parents indicate that "someday" they will get around to planning their estates;

- Your father once mentioned that he made a will, but no one knows if he really did;

- Your parents tells you that they drafted their wills themselves;

- Years ago you saw your parents' wills, but no one knows where they are now kept;

- Your parents indicate that they amended their wills, but the amendment is missing;

- Your mother's will refers to a trust, but the trust document cannot be found;

- Your parents mentioned they have a valuable stock certificate that you have never seen nor do you know the company;

- You are concerned that your parents have a taxable estate but do not possess the legal "know- how" to properly protect it; and

- Your parents tell you that the attorney who drafted their estate planning documents also kept the originals.

Each of the above scenarios is fraught with danger. Let us take some time to discover why.

The children of parents who say they will get around to planning their estates "someday" often discover too late that "someday" never came. It just kept being put off. Procrastination is the number one enemy of good estate planning.

Also, you can never be confident that your parents' estate plan is in place, despite their assurances, until you ask to see the documents yourself. Unfortunately, some parents reassure their children that their planning has been done merely as a way to avoid such a difficult discussion. Others feel that sharing the details of these documents with their children is "none of their business." Stock certificates that cannot be found are of zero value, however; as the saying goes, seeing is believing.

There is no way to judge the quality of your parents' estate plan without having an opportunity to examine the documents themselves. A good estate plan must be able to stand up against court challenges. Estate planning documents that are self-drafted, including those done with the assistance of some internet site, are done at the peril of the family. Wills are one of the most frequently contested documents in the country with many contests being successful. It therefore makes sense to ensure that your parents obtained professional help with the drafting of their estate planning documents. This is especially the case if your parents' estate is large enough to be subject to taxes. Planning estates to maximize everyone's legal right to pay the least amount of tax is not for amateurs.

You also need to make sure that you know where your parents' estate planning documents are kept, that they are secure, and that you can easily access them in an emergency. Lost estate planning documents are of no use to anyone. Documents that are not secure can be accidentally destroyed or even mysteriously disappear. Documents that are not easily available are of little use in an emergency.

The danger of not being able to find your parents' estate planning documents also exists if they indicate that their attorney has the originals. Attorneys sometimes move, retire, or die prior to their clients. We have had clients in the unfortunate position of not being able to retrieve the original documents from a former attorney who can no longer be found or whose client files have been destroyed. For this reason, you should be concerned if your parents indicate that they left their original estate planning documents with their attorney.

If you spot one of the above red flags in your discussion with your parents, now is the time to act. Take the steps necessary to encourage your parents to plan their estate. Putting it off until "someday" may prove to be too late!

How can I encourage my parents to plan?

If you have brought up the topic of estate planning with your parents only to be cut off with the response that "it's done" or "it's taken care of," do not let the discussion end there. Too much is at risk. You need to make sure they have a sound plan in place that is compatible with current law.

Even if they have a plan, you need to make sure it is up-to-date with the constantly changing circumstances of your family, as well as the law. Trusts, wills, and other legal documents should be reviewed and updated at least every two to three years to keep them current. You are doing your parents a favor by encouraging them to have their estate planning documents regularly reviewed.

By taking the following steps, you can promote a successful estate planning conversation with your parents:

- Pick a time and place that will be free of interruptions;

- Provide your parents with copies of this book and its companion publication, Your Life, Your Legacy: The Fundamentals of Effective Estate Planning, with the relevant sections highlighted, before you meet; and

- Prepare an agenda of discussion topics.

Consider the following events good opportunities to start the discussion:

- Your parents have just attended a funeral or visited a cemetery. You can say, "I really need to talk to you about what happens if you are not here anymore."

- When the issue of tax reform is seen in a newspaper or on the television, you may state, "I see there have been a lot of changes in the estate tax laws. Have you thought about how they affect your estate plan?"

- When you plan your own estate, tell your parents about it! Inform them about your plan and then inquire about theirs. Ask them if they are willing to discuss their plan with your attorney so your plan and theirs will work in tandem to best protect you and your children (their grandchildren).

Parents often say that everything is taken care of to avoid discussing this difficult topic, but if you wait for a crisis to occur before you insist on talking about it, it is usually too late. Planning done in a crisis is stressful, costs more, and limits your options for decision-making. Help your parents plan ahead to avoid this situation!

Even if your parents clearly have a plan in place, ask them whether an attorney who does only estate planning prepared it. The days are long past when the many complex issues involved with planning an estate could be entrusted to general practitioners who try to "do it all." This is not an area of the law in which an attorney should dabble. Many of the estate plans we review miss important planning opportunities or are just plain wrong. Let your parents know that it makes a lot of sense to get a second opinion of their documents from an attorney whose legal practice is dedicated to helping their clients plan their estates. Doing so will also help your parents overcome their resistance to planning their estate.

What if my parents still resist planning their estate?

If you are convinced that your parents understand the importance of planning their estate, but they still resist doing it, it is highly likely that your parents are afraid to plan. Such fears generally fall into two separate categories: First, some parents have the irrational, but nonetheless real, fear that planning their estate means they are going to die. They view it as if they are signing their own death warrant. Second, many parents resist planning their estates because they fear that by doing so they will surrender one of the most important things in their lives – control. They mistakenly assume that by planning their estate, they will give up legal control over their property and the other areas of their lives that they desperately want to retain for as long as possible. Maintaining control is as important, if not more important, to the elderly as it is to younger generations.

To help your parents overcome these fears, you need to approach them on a business-like level. If they are afraid that planning their estate is the equivalent of signing their death warrants, point out instances where others (their friends and maybe even yourself) planned their estates and kept enjoying life. Let them know that people who plan their estates say that it helped them sleep better because they now have the peace of mind of knowing they have taken care of this important task. Instead of something to fear, estate planning should be embraced as something that all thoughtful individuals do for themselves, their spouse, and their children.

If they fear that estate planning will force them to relinquish control over their lives, reassure them that a good estate plan will actually give them better control. Let them know that if they become disabled, the instructions in their trust can state their preference to stay at home, rather than being placed in a nursing home. Inform them that a good estate plan will also allow them to choose who will handle their finances and make medical decisions for them if they become disabled. Educate them that it is really those who do nothing who lose control because they are the ones who end up being wheeled into a court for a judge to decide their fate. Explain that a good estate plan can provide the surviving spouse with asset protection from lawsuits or protect children from the loss of their inheritance through a divorce. Alert them that a good estate plan will allow them to pass on what they have to whom they want, when they want, and how they want.

Many parents will respond to a proper presentation of the facts. Start with a simple heart-to-heart talk with your parents at their home. Then, with their permission, immediately pick up the telephone and schedule an appointment with a qualified estate planning attorney.

What planning issues should my parents consider?

In preparation for meeting with their estate planning attorney, your parents should consider the following issues:

- Where would they like to be taken care of if they are disabled? Would they like to stay at home? Would they prefer to stay with family members if possible? Would they prefer an assisted living facility rather than a nursing home? If so, their preferences need to be stated in their trust.

- Who will make health care decisions for them if they are disabled? Your parents need to consider who they want to have make decisions for them in a medical emergency. It should be someone who is capable of understanding medical issues and enforcing the care instructions that your parents state in their health care powers of attorney.

- Guardianship: Would they prefer to avoid a costly and public guardianship court proceeding to determine their mental competence and ability to handle their financial affairs? They can choose who they want to protect and manage their property without court involvement. They should decide if they want the other spouse, a trusted family member, a friend, a professional, or a combination of these together, to serve.

- Asset protection: Would they prefer the inheritance they leave to their spouse and children be protected from creditors and lawsuits in the event of a serious accident or other financial setback to the beneficiary? Asset protection can be achieved through a properly designed trust. If your parents want the inheritance left to loved ones to be asset protected, they need to incorporate appropriate provisions in their estate plan.

- Tax planning: Do they want to eliminate or minimize the impact of estate taxes? If they do, they need to be prepared to discuss the size of their estate and the investments and other assets that they have with the attorney.

- Remarriage protection: Are your parents concerned that their children (including you) could be disinherited because the surviving parent decides to remarry after one of them dies and leaves everything to the new spouse? A knowledgeable estate planning attorney can offer several solutions to keep the inheritance in the family.

- Divorce protection: Would your parents like to protect the inheritance left to you and your siblings in the event one of you goes through a divorce? If so, they should consider creating asset protection trusts for their children, since these types of trusts help put the inheritance beyond the reach of a predatory ex-spouse.

- Who will administer your parents' estate after they die? Selection of the person to handle the estate should be done thoughtfully. The job description consists of having a good financial head on one's shoulders and the ability to understand and perform the legal duties that come with this serious responsibility. When one spouse dies, it is often presumed that the other spouse will serve alone. Other options exist, such as having the surviving spouse and a child serve together. This can provide a surviving spouse with help to administer the estate and also gives the child an opportunity to learn about the ins and outs of handling the estate before the child has to do it all alone.

- Do they want to avoid probate? Although there is great confusion about this issue, the facts are simple: Wills guarantee probate; trusts can avoid probate. Your parents' estate planning attorney will be able to help them understand why this is the case and what is appropriate for them.

If your parents discuss these items ahead of time, they should be well-prepared when they meet with their estate planning attorney. With the information they provide, their attorney should be able to help them design a plan that not only protects them but also protects you and your siblings.

What if my parents want only a simple will that does not provide the legal protections that I feel are important for my siblings and me?

Although it might not be in the best interests of parents or the family, the choice of the type of an estate plan is frequently based simply on cost. The reality is that it costs more to include divorce and other asset protection planning into a trust than it does to draft a "simple" plan that leaves everything outright (no divorce or other asset protections) to the beneficiaries. If you are concerned that your parents are unwilling to pay the legal costs of providing you and your siblings the asset protections you feel are important, there are a couple of options that you might consider.

First, if your parents do not want to pay for the estate planning costs needed to protect the inheritance left to you and your siblings, you might offer to pay the extra cost yourself (or spread the cost out among you and your siblings). It is a wise child who is willing to pay a little up front to help his or her parents correctly plan their estates rather than doing nothing and having the entire inheritance jeopardized or lost.

A second way to protect your inheritance is to arrange for it to be placed directly into an "inheritor's trust." Your parents will name your inheritor's trust, instead of you, as the beneficiary of your inheritance. A knowledgeable estate planning attorney will build in the legal protections needed to guard your inheritance in case you are divorced or sued, as well as create a plan that minimizes taxation. This is typically a much better way to receive your inheritance than having it distributed to you outright and unprotected.

A new perspective!

If your parents have procrastinated in planning their estate, show them that estate planning, when done right, is not "death" planning but "life" planning. Help them understand that instead of surrendering control, a good estate plan will keep them in superior control of their lives. Who else will let them know that estate planning is planning for those you love? You have the opportunity and responsibility to your parents, your siblings, and yourself to help your parents put their estate in order.

Before you raise the topic of your parents' estate plan with them, it is a good idea to have completed your own planning. Not only will the fact that you planned your own estate give you a good reason to broach the topic with your parents, it will also put you in the positive position of showing them that you truly practice what you preach. This will prove to be one of the most important steps that you can take in helping your parents plan.

CHAPTER TEN

PROTECTING YOUR PETS

If you are like millions of others throughout the country, your pet is more than just an animal—it is part of your family! The 141 million dogs and cats living in U.S. homes provide affection, companionship, and undivided loyalty. It is only natural to want to return that affection by ensuring that your pet will continue to be taken care of when you can no longer do it yourself. That is why more and more pet owners are seeking to protect their pets by including provisions for them in their estate plan. It is not just dogs and cats that need special planning. The larger the animal, the more important it becomes to provide for their care. Many plans contain provisions to provide for horses and other large animals.

What options do I have if I want to protect my pets?

You have several options to consider if you want to protect your pets. Each has its pros and cons:

First, you can gift money to a trusted person with instructions that the money is to be used solely for the care of your pet. Many consider this the easiest and most expedient way to provide for your pet's future care, but you need to understand the risks that come with just giving money away. Once your money has changed hands, you lose complete control. It becomes the recipient's money, and there is no guarantee that it will be used for the intended purpose of taking care of your pet. It could be spent on anything the recipient considers more important than the needs of your pet, or despite the recipient's best intentions, the money could be lost in a lawsuit or other financial calamity.

Also, you do not know what will happen to your pet if the person who received the money becomes ill or dies. The custody of your pet could be transferred into unknown hands, and the money you gifted for your pet's care may pass to others or be used for the caregiver's needs. Finally, there is no guarantee that the person receiving the money will even be the one who receives custody of your pet. For these reasons, outright gifts are not the best way to ensure that the money you allocate for the care of your pet is actually used for that purpose.

Second, you can create a durable power of attorney to authorize your chosen agent to care for your pet if you become disabled. This option can provide the legal authority for your agent to receive both custody of your pet and the necessary legal authority to spend your money for your pet's care. In order for this alternative to work, your power of attorney must explicitly grant these powers.

Unfortunately, a power of attorney is not enough. All powers of attorney expire upon the maker's death. Therefore, your agent's authority to care for your pet ends upon your death. Providing for your pet's care following your death requires additional planning.

Third, you can draft a will that leaves instructions for your pet's care, but wills take legal effect only after the maker dies. You cannot use a will to plan for the protection of your pet in the event you become disabled. Accordingly, if you are considering planning with a will, you need two documents: a power of attorney to take care of your pet if you become disabled and a will to take care of your pet after you die.

Your pet will need immediate care after your death. A major disadvantage of trying to protect a pet with a will is the fact that no one has the legal authority to take possession of your pet or spend money for its care until the will is submitted into court and a judge appoints an executor. This can take several weeks or even months during which the fate of your pet is in limbo.

Another disadvantage of using a will is that, due to probate laws, the money allocated for your pet's care must be kept in a special trust known as a "testamentary trust." Since such testamentary trusts are under the probate court's continuing jurisdiction, your pet's caregiver will be forced to file annual reports and accountings with the probate court for as long as your pet lives. This is a big burden to place on someone who is doing you a favor by agreeing to look after your pet.

Your fourth and last option is to have your estate planning attorney include a "pet trust" in your revocable living trust, which serves to protect your pet no matter what happens to you. The instructions in your revocable living trust take effect immediately when signed, and those instructions remain in effect even if you become disabled or die. Unlike the instructions in a power of attorney, the directives in your trust do not expire upon your death and are free of probate court supervision. The successor trustee assumes authority immediately upon your incapacity or death. This means that the person you select as the successor trustee of your revocable living trust takes immediate legal custody of your pet and can expend any money necessary for its care without permission from anyone else. Also, since your revocable living trust is not subject to probate court supervision, your trustee need not file any reports or accountings as is demanded for those who are appointed to administer testamentary trusts.

Your pet trust will contain instructions that legally authorize and instruct your trustee to pay for your pet's housing, veterinary care, and other expenses. Your pet trust can even require the trustee to review the living conditions of your pet to ensure that it is being taken care of by the assigned caretaker according to your standards. Your trustee will also maintain supervision over the money so it is not "lost" if it becomes necessary to change caretakers. The trust can additionally state who will receive any trust assets left over after your pet is gone.

Because of the many advantages of including a pet trust in your revocable living trust, we believe it the best option for those who want to designate a caretaker, leave instructions for your pet's care, and reserve the financial resources necessary to pay for that care.

What should I consider when planning for my pet?

There are many important issues that should be considered if you seek to protect a pet, including:

- The type of care that your pet requires and the standards that you desire to be followed for its care;

- The amount of money that you believe is necessary or appropriate to provide for your pet's care;

- The selection of the caregiver;

- The selection of a successor caregiver if the first is unable to serve;

- Whether the caretaker (the person with custody of your pet) and the trustee (the person who handles the money for your pet's care) should be the same individual or whether different individuals should be appointed; and

- Which individuals or charities should receive any remaining trust funds once your pet has passed away.

If you want to make sure that your beloved pet is properly cared for if you are no longer able to do so yourself, then you need to put a solid plan into place. An experienced estate planning attorney who has helped others protect their pets can help you set the wheels in motion.

CHAPTER ELEVEN

WHEN LAND IS A LEGACY

One of the most cherished and valuable possessions that we can leave to our families is the land that we own. Whether it is a residence, the family cottage, hunting land, the farm, or a vacation timeshare, there is always something special about land. First of all, land is unique; there are no two pieces exactly alike. Second, land is valuable – often the most valuable asset we own. Third, many of our most important memories are tied to specific parcels of land; we have special memories of where we were raised and where we spent our vacations. Fourth, land often acts as a touchstone that ties the generations of a family together. Land is a legacy that can be passed from one generation to the next.

Accordingly, care should be taken to protect and preserve this special property when the time comes to transfer it to your children or next of kin. Remember: failure to properly plan may result in the loss of the family legacy.

What can cause property to be lost at a time of transfer?

Here are some ways property can be lost when it is transferred from one generation to the next:

- Poor titling of the property;

- Poor timing of the transfer;

- Poorly understood tax laws that act as traps that snare the unwary; and

- Poor family dynamics.

This chapter is written in order to help you make sure that the baton is not dropped when your family passes land from one generation to the next.

What is important about how property is titled?

All good estate planning depends on holding and transferring proper title. "Title" is the term that is used to describe the property owner, how it is owned, and the extent of ownership. Understanding how the title to property works is critical if you want to correctly pass your land on to the next generation. You can give your property away only if you own it, or, in other words, have legal "title" to it.

Can you give an example of how a person's desire to transfer property can be ignored based on how it is titled?

Consider this scenario: a person owns a cottage or hunting land with others as joint tenants. Each owner understands that everyone named as a joint tenant on the deed to the property has an equal right to use the property. What some may fail to understand, however; is that joint tenants do not have the right to leave their interest in the land to others after they die. The property interest terminates the second one joint tenant dies; any remaining joint tenants continue to own the property. If only one joint tenant remains alive, then that person owns it all.

We have seen tragic situations where the surviving spouse or children of such joint tenants thought they were inheriting an interest in a family cottage or parcel of hunting land according to the terms laid out in the deceased's will, but since the title trumps the will, the surviving joint tenant gets the property. The family gets nothing.

The same situation can occur when a surviving parent puts one of the children on the deed to the house as a joint tenant. This is sometimes done as a way to avoid probate or because of a concern that the house will be lost if nursing home care becomes necessary. The parent failed to understand how joint tenancy works, and as a consequence, the named child gets the entire house; the others get nothing. This is true even if the parent's will states that the children should inherit the house equally.

It is very important to understand how title works in order to make sure that your family receives the property that you want to leave to them in exactly the way that you want them to receive it. Your estate planning attorney can help you sort out these types of title issues so you can be assured that your desires are carried out instead of ignored due to a poor understanding of the law.

How does the poor timing of a transfer cause a family to lose its property?

One of the most important considerations in leaving your property to others is the timing of the transfer. If you transfer your land too soon, your children might not have the maturity or financial resources to maintain and preserve it. Also, since children are the most susceptible to divorces, creditor problems, and lawsuits when they are younger, transferring it too soon could precipitously expose the property to any of these dangers.

What are the tax traps to be avoided?

Another disadvantage of transferring property (gifting it) to the children too soon is that it can create a tax trap for the unwary. There may be gift taxes due if the property exceeds the available gift tax exemptions, and the children may have to pay capital gains taxes when the property is sold that could have been avoided. Property that is received as a gift does not get the valuable step-up in tax basis that is available when property is received as an inheritance.

Suppose you bought property twenty years ago for $20,000

that is now worth $220,000. If you give the property to your children during your lifetime, you must account for the gift tax using the value of $220,000, but the children receive your tax basis of $20,000. If your children sell the property after it has been transferred to them for $220,000, they will pay capital gains tax on the entire $200,000 gain. Ouch!

If your children inherit the property from you following your death, their tax basis will be the property's fair market value at the time of your death. When the property is sold, they will pay capital gains tax only on any increase in its value after your death. If there is little or no gain, they pay little or no capital gains tax.

When children are forced to pay capital gains taxes, it can have a huge impact on their ability to preserve a prized piece of land. Often parents will give several parcels of land to their children thinking that the sale of some of the land will provide the cash their children need to protect the prized parcel. Unfortunately, the amount the children receive from the sale, after paying capital gains taxes, may be significantly less than what the parents expected, leaving the children without enough assets to protect the prized parcel and preserve the legacy. As you can see, the timing of whether a transfer occurs during your life or following your death can make a huge difference.

Despite these dangers of transferring property too soon, there are some advantages to transferring property to your family while you are still alive. One is that it can give you the joy of seeing your children and grandchildren benefit from the property.

Further, there may actually be a possible tax benefit to giving property away before you die. This tax advantage can occur if the property is rapidly appreciating in value and your estate is subject to death taxes. By giving property that is rapidly appreciating, you remove it from your taxable estate and transfer the future growth of value to the next generation.

Still another potential advantage to a lifetime transfer is that, if done right, the property can be protected from the expenses of a catastrophic illness, or an extended nursing home stay. Again, the timing of this type of planning is critical. In order to protect your property from such costs, it must be transferred well in advance of the illness to avoid the divestment penalties discussed in Chapter Eight. An experienced estate planning attorney can help you calculate the best time to transfer your property.

How can property be lost as a consequence of poor family dynamics?

Our clients universally tell us that they want their estate plan to promote peace and harmony among their children, but whenever there is more than one person involved, the potential for conflict exists – especially in regard to the family legacy.

Assume the following common scenario: a parent leaves the cherished family cottage to three children with the intent that someday the grandchildren will inherit it. After the parent dies, the child who lives the closest to the cottage loves it and uses it the most. Another has other interests and uses it infrequently. The third has moved far away from the cottage and has no interest in it whatsoever. This situation is ripe for conflict.

Children who own an interest in such property, but who use it seldom or not at all, are generally not overly enthusiastic about being asked to pay for insurance and property taxes or to help out with maintenance costs when the roof needs replacing. If times get tight for them due to economic times, creditor problems, a divorce, or a lawsuit, they may want (or be forced) to sell their interest in the property. If the other family members cannot finance the purchase, the land is lost.

Even if the grandchildren ultimately inherit by the cottage, they may for the most part be strangers to each other (especially if they grew up in different parts of the country). If siblings have a hard time maintaining the property, how will cousins fare? The chances are considerable that one or more of the grandchildren might not even want to own the cottage. The consequence: a forced sale of the property occurs.

One way to minimize such future conflicts is to simply discuss the issue with your family. Ask your children about their interest in the land and their desire for ownership. This important option is often overlooked and can yield surprising and valuable information. If only one child really wants the property, there might be a way to design the estate plan so that the one child gets the cottage, while the remaining children receive equitable compensation from alternative assets.

How can I leave my vacation property to one of my children yet still be fair to the others?

There are several options available: one is to try equalizing your children's inheritances by directing other assets to the children who are not getting the vacation property. Another option might be to purchase a life insurance policy that will provide an equivalent amount of cash for the other children following your death. Still another option is to allow the child who wants the property to purchase it from you right away or from your estate following your death. Your child may even purchase a life insurance policy on your life so that the buy-out money is available.

In order to determine which option makes the most sense for your family, you first need to sit down with the children and discuss what they want. Then, with the knowledge you gain from these conversations, you and your estate planning attorney can design a creative solution that promotes peace and harmony for everyone.

What if I truly want to keep the property in my family for generations?

You know from experience that the purchase price of your cherished getaway was just the beginning of its costs. You know that there are ongoing maintenance costs, insurance premiums, and property taxes to be paid. If you intend for several generations of your descendants to have access to the property, you need to explore a very important issue: how will all these generations be able to collectively pay for it? It is not good planning to just leave them the property and say, "good luck." You need to figure out in advance how the use of the property will be governed and how the expenses will be paid. If you family is left to wrangle through these issues on its own, you are creating a headache for them and taking the fun out of the property.

Issues will always arise with respect to the use, management, and care of the property, but proactively preparing a way for the next generation to reach amicable solutions will help promote and maintain family harmony. Essential to this is establishing a workable decision-making process.

The first major issue that needs resolving is how will your family members pay for everything? Will they be required to pay annual dues? If yes, then who will determine how much each person owes, and how will the dues be assessed and collected?

There are various legal ways to structure such decision-making. A partnership could be formed wherein each family member partner gets a vote, but this can be unwieldy if there are several individuals involved. Also, if a majority of the partners want to sell the property, the majority rules.

Another potential solution is to create a family limited partnership that owns the land. Limited partnerships have two types of partners. First are the "limited partners." Limited partners get to share in the use of the property according to the partnership agreement, as well as share any proceeds if the property is sold. Limited partners have no say in the management of the property.

The second type of partner is called "general partner." General partners have the sole right to manage the partnership. Because limited partnerships place the management of a legacy property in the hands of a few trusted individuals, they can work well in families that have members with good management skills. In large families, there can be a representative of each family serving as a general partner.

Another option to assist future generations in managing a parcel of legacy property is to create a trust. In many instances, a trust will provide a better solution for dealing with these decision-making issues than will an outright distribution of the asset to your family or the creation of a partnership.

First, trusts can be designed with detailed instructions concerning the long-term management of a legacy property. Second, not everyone in the family may have the talent, time, or desire to deal with all the decision-making headaches involved. Such responsibilities can entail scheduling usage, paying utilities, overseeing normal maintenance, deciding on major repairs, and other such ownership responsibilities. Your trust instructions can appoint your hand-picked trustees to handle these issues. It is wise to free those who are ill equipped to handle these maintenance issues by placing the responsibility on family members who are better able to manage them, while still guaranteeing that everyone has an equal right to enjoy the property.

Second, trusts are the ideal legal tool to use when property is to be kept in the family for generations. This is because your trust instructions can establish how successor trustees will be chosen to replace the original trustees when they are no longer able to serve. The value of having an orderly trustee succession to oversee the long-term management of your legacy property cannot be overstated.

What else should I know about creating a legacy in my property for future generations?

In addition to ensuring the wise future management of your property, you should also consider the wisdom of making sure the funds exist to preserve it. In other words, instead of placing the bill paying responsibility on the next generation, the best solution is to design your estate plan so that the majority of expenses are handled directly by your trust. This is an important issue to consider because a family that cannot afford the property cannot retain the property.

If your estate has sufficient assets, you can fund your trust with an endowment for the property's ongoing expenses. This will guarantee that your loved ones not only inherit the property, but have funding in place to keep it in the family perpetually.

Alternatively, if your estate does not have the assets needed to fund such an endowment, an option is to purchase a life insurance policy that will provide the liquidity to fund the endowment after your passing. If this option is not available to you, other potential solutions should be considered.

What other estate planning solutions are available to me to keep the property in my family?

Some families who desire to make a lifetime gift of property to their children are appropriately concerned about the gift tax ramifications of those transfers. If this is a concern for you, you might consider giving small interests in the property over an extended period of time directly to your family, to your family limited partnership, or to your trust that holds the legacy property. This strategy will allow you to take full advantage of the annual gift tax exclusion to slowly, but surely, move the property to the next generation free of gift and estate taxes.

Are there other ways to transfer my property to my family?

Another option for those who want to consider a lifetime transfer of their property is to sell it to family members who want it rather than leaving it to your family upon your death. A sale might be the best solution—especially if you need the sale proceeds for your retirement years. Also, if you decide to sell the property to family members, you can choose whether the sale will be outright or completed on an installment basis.

Remember: the sale may be subject to capital gains taxes but there are estate planning strategies available to help you minimize or avoid them.

What if I retain a life estate interest?

A life estate is created when you deed legal ownership of the property to your family but retain the right to use the property for the rest of your life. Although you technically surrender the property's ownership, you still are entitled to the beneficial enjoyment of the property. You continue to decide how the property is used and who has the right to use it. It is only on your death that the right of ownership, called the "remainder interest," passes from you to your family.

This is an excellent transfer strategy to use in situations where an outright gift of the property is not advised because family members have financial trouble or a bad marriage. In such situations, a gift of the property could expose it to the claims of your family member's creditors or a subsequent divorcing spouse. By retaining a life estate, you keep complete control of the property during your lifetime.

Maintaining a life estate can also provide an important tax advantage. Your property will realize a step-up in tax basis to fair market value on your death.

You should also be aware that there are potential disadvantages to a life estate. If you want to sell the property, you must obtain the signatures of those family members to whom you have given the remainder interest on the deed. Also, unless your planning is done carefully, these types of transfers can cause gift and estate tax issues. Additionally, if you apply for Medicaid, the value of you life estate will be taken into account.

Are there any additional transfer options that I need to know about?

With special planning, you might be able to shield your residence or vacation home from estate taxes. To do this you need to transfer your home into a special trust known as a Qualified Personal Residence Trust, or "QPRT." The tax laws concerning QPRTs are rather complex, so if you want to explore this option, you should consult a knowledgeable estate planning attorney.

Another option to consider when transferring a prized piece of property to your family, and at the same time preserveing its pristine nature for future generations, is to grant a conservation easement. Conservation easements place development restrictions on the use of property. For example, 40 acres of wooded lake front property could be restricted to one single family home, or you could agree not to mine the land or harvest the timber. By placing conservation easements on your land, not only will you be helping to keep it pristine, you will also be potentially helping yourself with attractive income, gift, and estate tax deductions.

How can I provide for changing circumstances?

Family circumstances change. Births and deaths occur, people get older, move away, or want to sell out. Changes in health, finances, and relationships occur. Few people can confidently predict today what their family situation will look like in twenty years. For this reason, it makes sense to build flexibility into any transfer of special property. Your estate planning attorney will be able to help you design a plan that accomplishes your goals while retaining the maximum flexibility necessary to modify your plan due to changing circumstances.

Bottom line: if you have a special asset that you want to keep in the family, a special plan is needed. Start your planning by discussing these issues with your family. Then, share this knowledge and your goals with your estate planning attorney, who is equipped with the expertise to provide you with effective options that will accomplish your specific needs. With careful planning, you truly can create a legacy in the land.

CHAPTER TWELVE

INTEGRATING RETIREMENT ACCOUNTS WITH YOUR ESTATE PLAN

Qualified retirement accounts now comprise a substantial portion of many estates, and more and more people are depending on these savings to provide for their lifestyle after their working careers end. When we talk about qualified retirement accounts, we include all types of retirement plans, such as IRA, 401K, 403(B), and 457 accounts, to name a few of the most common types of retirement savings funds. For simplicity, we will refer to all of these accounts as IRAs throughout this chapter.

Key to the attractiveness of IRAs is the ability of individuals to take advantage of income tax rules that allow their IRA assets to grow tax deferred. When untaxed assets are invested and allowed to compound over several decades, spectacular growth can occur. For many individuals, the value of their IRA comprises the single largest asset they own, even exceeding the value of their home. While a large IRA is beneficial for the owner, it can be a very troublesome asset for estate-planning purposes.

As estate planning attorneys, we are meeting more and more clients with sizeable IRAs. During our estate planning conferences, we learn that many clients, based upon their lifestyles and life expectancies, will likely never use all of the assets in their IRA, even though IRA rules require that minimum annual withdrawals be made. This scenario has both good and bad consequences for you and your family. The good news is that the IRA will serve its purpose: it will provide the financial resources you need to maintain your lifestyle during your retirement.

Now for the bad news: The assets left in your IRA following your death may be subject to quadruple taxation! According to The Wall Street Journal, these taxes can diminish an IRA by more than 80% before it passes to a beneficiary. After this draconian tax hit, there may be little left of your IRA to pass on to your children or other beneficiaries.

Assume you contribute to your IRA your entire life and build up a sizable account. Upon retirement, you take distributions to pay for your living needs. You calculate that at your death there will still be $100,000.00 in your account to leave to your loved ones, but if your IRA is taxed at 80%, your loved ones will receive only $20,000.00—a fraction of what you thought they would inherit. If you think this is awful, we agree; and these results are avoidable. Your IRA can be one of the most powerful and valuable assets you own if it is properly integrated into your estate plan.

Why is special planning needed?

      The rules that apply to IRAs during your lifetime are technical and complex, and they become even more so if you want to leave your IRA to your children or other beneficiaries after your death. If the value of your IRA is to be preserved, special planning is essential to ensure compliance with the latest regulations, which include:

- Early withdrawal penalties;

- Minimum mandatory distribution rules that are different for you, your spouse, and your other beneficiaries;

- A 50% penalty for a late withdrawal;

- State and federal income taxation for the owner;

- Different state and federal income tax rules for beneficiaries;

- Distributions to a disabled child;

- Different "rollover" rights for owners, spouses, and beneficiaries;

- Avoiding exposure of inherited IRA assets to creditor claims and lawsuits;

- Difficulties in designating proper beneficiaries; and

- Different rules for different types of IRAs.

Ignoring any of these rules can decimate the value of your IRA. To avoid the minefield of tax and investment traps and take full advantage of the available planning opportunities, you need the help of an estate planning team consisting of an experienced estate planning attorney, accountant, and financial advisor.

When can I withdraw money from my IRA?

You may make lifetime withdrawals from your IRA at any time regardless of your age, but any amount withdrawn will constitute taxable income in the year of the withdrawal. You may also be required to pay an additional penalty tax equal to 10% of the amount that is withdrawn if you are younger than 59 ½ at the time of the withdrawal. If you find yourself facing this penalty, contact your estate planning attorney and financial planner to determine if you quality for one of the exceptions.

Do I have to take withdrawals from my IRA?

While IRA assets are tax deferred, they are not tax-free. Sooner or later the IRS regulations force you to take withdrawals from your IRA, and income taxes must then be paid to the federal government as well as your state government if your state of residence has an income tax. A key IRA-planning strategy is to defer these taxes as long as possible by taking the least amount permitted and by not taking withdrawals until the last possible moment.

When must I begin taking withdrawals from my IRA?

If you are no longer working, you must take your first IRA

withdrawal the year in which you reach age 70 ½ (the first distribution year). Annual distributions must then be taken for each subsequent year. All withdrawals must be taken by December 31st of each calendar year (except for the first distribution year in which you may delay your withdrawal until April 1st of the year following the year you turn 70 ½).

How much must I take out?

IRS regulations require you to take a specific amount from your IRA. This amount is known as the "required minimum distribution" (RMD). Your RMD is calculated based on the size of your IRA and your life expectancy. The custodian of your IRA calculates the value of your IRA on January 1st of each year, and the IRS publishes a table identifying the fraction of the IRA value that must be withdrawn.

What happens if I withdraw more than the RMD in any year?

If you withdraw more than your required minimum distribution for a given year, you simply pay the income taxes on the amount withdrawn. There is no penalty for withdrawing more than is required from your IRA.

What is the withdrawal rule if I own more than one IRA?

If you have multiple IRAs, you need to compute the RMD for each IRA and then add them together. So long as you remember to do this, you can withdraw the total required amount from any one or more of your IRA accounts.

What if I forget to withdraw the RMD?

If you forget to withdraw your RMD, you must pay an additional penalty tax that is equal to 50% of the shortfall (i.e. the amount of the RMD that you were required to withdraw but did not). To avoid the penalty, you must withdraw at least the RMD from your IRA every year, even in the year you die. This requirement frequently catches executors of estates by surprise, and they fail to take the withdrawal. When this happens, the executor can be held personally liable for any taxes owed plus the 50% penalty. Consequently, it is very important that the RMD always be taken.

What if I become mentally disabled and cannot take my RMD?

If you are older than 70 ½ and become mentally disabled, your RMD must still be withdrawn. If you cannot do it yourself, the obligation will fall on the person appointed to handle legal matters for you.

If you have a durable power of attorney in place, your representative will be the agent you named.

If you do not have a power of attorney, or if your power of attorney does not authorize your agent to make withdrawals from your retirement account, it may be necessary for someone to open formal guardianship proceedings in probate court. That person (usually, but not necessarily, a family member) will need to file a petition with the court to have you declared incompetent. That person will also need to petition the court to be appointed your legal guardian and receive authority to handle your financial matters.

Once appointed, the guardian will have the legal authority to make decisions regarding your property, including your IRAs. Since guardianship court proceedings are emotionally trying, costly to pursue, and take months to complete, it makes sense for everyone to take the steps needed to avoid them. You can help your family avoid guardianship proceedings by having a durable power of attorney that gives your agent broad authority to take many actions on your behalf throughout your incapacity, including taking your RMD withdrawals for you. Please note that the agent's authority to handle your IRA will exist only while you are alive, since your agent's legal authority to act on your behalf ends upon your death.

What happens to my IRA after I die?

After you die, the assets in your IRA are subject to federal as well as state estate tax (if your state of residence taxes estates). The IRA is then distributed to the legal beneficiaries.

Who are the legal beneficiaries of my IRA?

- The beneficiaries you named in the written beneficiary designation form filed with the IRA custodian;

- The default beneficiaries named in the IRA custodian agreement, if you failed to designate your own beneficiaries; or

- Your probate estate, if the beneficiaries designated by you and those specified in the IRA custodian agreement predecease you.

If you want control over who will receive your IRA assets following your death, you need to designate your own beneficiaries. Otherwise, the IRA may go to the default beneficiaries named in the IRA custodian agreement, which could well be your probate estate.

By naming your own IRA beneficiaries, your IRA assets will be distributed directly to your beneficiaries free of the incumbent costs, delays, and other problems that can result from probate court involvement. For this reason, it is very important to regularly review your IRA beneficiary designations. You want to make sure that the beneficiaries named are accurate and that the percentage of your IRA that you want each to receive after your death is correctly stated.

While having your IRA account distributed directly to your designated beneficiaries is typically desirable, you must be aware of estate taxes. If your estate, which includes the IRA, owes estate taxes at the time of your death, your estate plan needs to identify who pays the tax. Assume you name your children as the beneficiaries of your IRA and your spouse as the beneficiary of the balance of your estate. Since the IRA passes directly to your beneficiaries, the tax on the IRA will be paid by your estate, which now belongs to your spouse. After paying the estate taxes, your spouse may have a substantially lesser estate than you intended.

Who should I consider as the beneficiary of my IRA?

Who you name as the beneficiary of your IRA depends on your personal planning goals. Possible beneficiaries include:

- Your spouse

- Your children

- Other loved ones

- Trust

- Charities

You should carefully consider whom you name as the beneficiary of your IRA because there are distinct tax consequences for each choice.

What if my spouse is my beneficiary?

Because spouses have certain preferred tax elections that are unavailable to any other beneficiary, spouses receive the best income tax treatment under the Internal Revenue Code. The most important of these elections permits your spouse to roll your IRA into an IRA owned solely by your spouse. This is known as a "spousal rollover" IRA.

The tax benefits of a spousal rollover can be huge. If your surviving spouse is younger than you, your spouse can use his or her own age to determine the required beginning date for the mandatory minimum distributions. In other words, your spouse can keep your IRA assets tax deferred until your spouse reaches the mandatory distribution age. This can extend the period of tax deferred growth of your IRA for several years.

Who gets my IRA after my spouse dies?

The answer to this question depends upon the plan in which the IRA funds are invested. Many people assume if the IRA stays in your name with benefits payable to your spouse, then the IRA will be paid to the contingent beneficiaries you name after your spouse dies. This is typically not true. Some plans permit your spouse to name a new beneficiary. When your spouse dies, the beneficiary named by your spouse steps into your spouse's shoes as the new owner of the account. However, many plans do not allow your spouse to name a new beneficiary when your IRA remains in your name. As a result, the IRA proceeds would be paid to your spouse's estate or to the default beneficiary (if there is one) named by the plan. IRAs payable to an estate lose the stretch-out privilege and IRAs payable to a successor beneficiary, when permitted, must use the life expectancy of the spouse.

Your spouse has a second option concerning your IRA. Your spouse may transfer or rollover your IRA to his or her own IRA. Your spouse then becomes the new owner and may designate new primary and contingent beneficiaries. These beneficiaries are now entitled to stretch-out the IRA payments for the life expectancy of the beneficiary.

Is it necessary to name contingent beneficiaries if I name a primary one?

Every owner of an IRA should always designate one or more primary beneficiaries and one or more contingent beneficiaries to receive any remaining IRA assets. Contingent beneficiaries should be named so there is always someone who will receive the IRA if the primary beneficiary dies before you do. If a beneficiary is not designated, the remaining IRA assets will generally be payable to the owner's probate estate. This could have disastrous tax and estate administration consequences, especially if your IRA ends up being distributed to someone other than your spouse.

What happens if I leave my IRA to someone other than my spouse?

All non-spouse beneficiaries, including children, must begin taking required minimum distributions by December 31st of the year following the owner's death. This rule applies to all non-spouse beneficiaries regardless of age. The required minimum distribution is calculated based on the size of the IRA and the age of the beneficiary.

Non-spouse beneficiaries can withdraw any or all of the inherited IRA at any time, regardless of their age, without paying any penalties; income taxes, however, must be paid on any and all IRA withdrawals. If the beneficiary withdraws all of the IRA, income taxes must be paid on the entire amount. This is rarely a good idea because tax deferred growth is lost and the large amount of income taxes that must be immediately paid greatly reduces the earning power of the account. Instead, it is a much better strategy for a beneficiary to "stretch out" withdrawals so that the tax hit is spread out for the longest time possible.

What is a "Stretch IRA"?

A Stretch IRA, sometimes referred to as a "Stretch-out IRA," is not a different type of IRA. It is simply a description of how the beneficiary elects to receive an inherited IRA. If the beneficiary takes only the RMD each year, the IRA has been stretched.

How can I stretch out my inherited IRA for the longest time possible?

A beneficiary can stretch out an inherited IRA by withdrawing only the minimum required distribution each year. The remaining assets in the IRA will grow tax-free until the next required minimum distribution. Doing this will give the beneficiary the extraordinary opportunity to obtain tax deferred compounded growth of the IRA's assets. Since tax deferred compounded growth can easily multiply the value of the inheritance over the lifetime of the beneficiary, this is an opportunity that should not be overlooked.

If you want your beneficiaries to stretch-out the IRA they inherit from you, you should have an experienced estate planning attorney determine the best way to achieve this result. Among other technical requirements, the attorney will need to make sure that any estate debts, taxes, or other expenses due as a result of your death are not paid from your IRA. You should also consider including provisions in your plan to prevent your beneficiaries from withdrawing the IRA faster than required.

What happens when a beneficiary is a minor?

Since a minor lacks legal capacity, the IRA custodian may require that a court appoint a guardian before any IRA distributions can be made. Even the parent of a minor may have to be appointed by the court as the guardian for the child. Guardianship proceedings can be time consuming and expensive, plus there are ongoing costs due to annual reports that must be filed with the Probate Court. The guardian must also be bonded. These problems can be avoided by creating a trust with special provisions to hold any IRAs or other assets left to a minor.

Can a trust be named as an IRA beneficiary?

Yes, as long as the trust complies with the IRS's "designated beneficiary" regulations, and this takes special drafting. Trusts can be extremely useful in managing the IRA assets that you leave to your loved ones. Your trust can limit distributions to the RMD amount until your beneficiary reaches a designated age. Your trust can also contain instructions to guide the investment and expenditure of IRA assets for minors, disabled beneficiaries, or spendthrift beneficiaries who do not have the experience or skill to wisely manage inherited assets. Trusts can also protect your beneficiary from losing the IRA due to a failed marriage, creditor claim, or lawsuit, as well as minimize estate taxes in the beneficiary's estate.

Great caution is needed when naming a trust as the beneficiary of an IRA. Not every trust will qualify or permit stretch-out treatment, which means income taxes on the IRA will have to be paid sooner rather than later, and your loved ones will miss out on benefiting from the tax deferred compounded growth of their inherited IRA assets.

Should I name my living trust as the owner of my IRA?

No! Unlike most of your other assets, the ownership (title) of your IRA should never be transferred to your revocable living trust during your lifetime. The IRS treats the transfer of ownership of your IRA in any manner, including to a living trust, as a withdrawal. This means income taxes are immediately due on the entire IRA! While a trust can be named as a beneficiary of your IRA, it should never be named as its owner. A trust should not even be named as a beneficiary unless the trust is drafted to comply with the IRS's designated beneficiary rules.

When should I review my IRA beneficiary designations?

Now! Beneficiary designations form a significant part of any estate plan and, in many instances, they control where the majority of the estate will be distributed when the owner dies. Accordingly, just as your estate plan needs regular review, so do your beneficiary designations. When you review your beneficiary designations, check that all of the following are done:

- The beneficiary designation form correctly states who you want to be the primary beneficiaries of your IRA and what percentage of its assets you want each primary beneficiary to receive;

- Your beneficiary designation form correctly states who you want to be the contingent (secondary) beneficiaries of your IRA and what percentage of its assets you want each contingent beneficiary to receive;

- You have received a copy of the beneficiary form for your own records and placed a copy in your trust portfolio or safely secured it in a place that is accessible to the person who is going to administer your estate; and

- Make sure the IRA custodian has provided written confirmation to you that the form has been processed and accepted.

Each of the above steps is necessary to ensure that your desires as to who will inherit your IRA are carried out. It is not enough to just fill out the form. You need to make sure that the custodian has received your beneficiary designation and that it is acceptable to the IRA administrator. We have seen situations where the custodian loses the beneficiary form and then takes the position that no beneficiary was ever designated because it has no form in its files. If your records contain a confirmation from the IRA custodian acknowledging that your IRA beneficiary designation was processed and accepted, your loved ones have the proof they need to receive your IRA the way you intended.

It is important to carefully plan who will receive your IRA after your death. By properly naming a trust as a beneficiary, you can also make sure that your loved ones will not only receive legal protection from creditors, lawsuits, and failed marriages when they inherit your IRA, but they will also have the opportunity to minimize the tax bite on the IRA while simultaneously achieving maximum tax deferred compounded growth. This is the type of legacy you can leave your loved ones when you take the opportunity to proactively plan for your IRAs as a critical part of your overall estate plan.

CHAPTER THIRTEEN

KEEPING YOUR FAMILY FARM OR BUSINESS IN THE FAMILY

In January 2012, the first baby-boomers reached their full Social Security retirement age which signaled the start of the greatest transition of ownership of family owned businesses, including farms, in American history. Many entrepreneurs rely on their businesses for their personal retirements and also want their lifetime work passed on to their children so that the family business will continue. Unfortunately, history shows us that most family business transitions fail. Successful business transitions are more likely to occur if the business owner and children approach the transition in a thoughtful and fair manner.

What are the Statistics?

Family owned businesses are vital to the American economy. Approximately 95 percent of U.S. corporations are closely held and account for over one-half of the gross national product, as well as 50 percent of the total wages paid, according to Internal Revenue statistics. While nearly 70 percent of the owners of family owned businesses indicate their desire to have the business be transitioned to family members, only 27 percent of these owners have established a formal business succession plan. In addition, business owners have 37 percent of their net worth tied up in their business, and this percentage is generally much higher for farmers. Because the business owner needs to get value out of the business to finance retirement, it is usually not possible to simply give the business to the family member successors. The family business successors typically have no financial resources to buy the parents' interest. A monetary strain is placed on the business if a sale transpires because the business must now create revenue to pay the purchase price to the original owner plus support the new owner. Is it any wonder that less than 30 percent of family businesses pass successfully to the next generation, and less than 13 percent of family businesses stay in the family for over 60 years?

This is not a small problem. The Small Business Administration reports that 40 percent of U.S. businesses are facing a transfer of ownership at any given time, and the primary cause for failure is lack of planning. Family businesses are vital to the U.S. economy, and owners need to be aware of what it takes for the family business to be successfully transferred.

What are the benefits of planning?

The most common benefits a business owner achieves through planning for a transition include:

- An orderly process that is known to family members so that disputes are minimized and known to vendors and customers so that business is retained.

- The maximization of value from the business.

- Assurance that the business has the greatest likelihood of success after transition.

- The preservation of wealth for the family.

What conflicts exist in a business transition?

To understand the potential conflicts, you must first understand the interrelationship of the people involved. Some are family members, some are owners, and some are employed by the business. Complications and disputes can arise particularly with those who hold multiple positions. There are inherent conflicts among the various positions, and a successful plan must deal with all of these positions and potential conflicts. A discussion of the various positions will help identify why planning is essential.

First Position

This person is a family member but not an owner or employee of the business. Commonly, each child wants to be treated equally with the other children at time of inheritance. If one child is given the business or allowed to buy the business at a below market price, the other children will receive far less value as their inheritance. Business owners know that the business has a limit on the amount of debt it can handle and may believe the successor child needs special consideration as to price to keep the business profitable. This frequently results in resentment from the children not in the business.

Second Position

This person is an owner but not in the family nor in the business. Many family businesses were started by related parties (i.e. siblings) or close friends. Perhaps an investor helped provide the start-up capital and retains an ownership interest. Upon the death of the investor, the investor's children retain ownership interests but no business participation. The investor or the investor's heirs are concerned about their rate of return on investment. This conflicts with the owner's goal of reinvesting profits in the business for future growth.

Third Position

This person is in business but is not in the family, nor an owner. Key employees fall into this category. The Company needs to keep the key employees, but while the key employees have been fiercely loyal to the original owner, they may not have the same feelings for the successor.

Fourth Position

This person is in the family and a business owner but not working in the business. This typically occurs when a child inherits ownership but already has his or her own employment and no desire to be actively involved in the business. Even though this person is not in the business there is still an interest in receiving a good rate of return or the ownership interest and perhaps even sitting on the Board of Directors. The child running the business wants to reinvest the earnings into the business for growth rather than making distributions of the earnings to siblings who played no part in creating the earnings. This owner child also wants the unfettered control of the business and many resent siblings sitting on the Board of Directors.

Fifth Position

This person is an owner and employee of the business but is not in the family. This person is concerned about the ability of the Company to survive the transition to the next generation and how the transition will affect the historic income flow of the Company. There is also concern about working with a new generation of owners.

Sixth Position

This person is in the family and works for the business but has no ownership interest. Perhaps the future owner of the company falls into this category or perhaps a sibling purchased the business, and this person never got the chance to be an owner. Earnings are limited to wages paid while the owner sibling enjoys the profits of the Company.

Seventh Position

The last position holds ownership, works in the business, and is a family member. This person has it all but may also be the target of jealousies from the other six positions. This person must also be a successful business leader to ensure that the Company remains successful. When a child is transitioned into this position, he or she must be able to run the Company in a profitable manner, pay a fair price to the parent, support his or her own family, and resolve issues with the other six positions that have conflicting viewpoints.

A successful transition plan must deal with all of these varying roles and potential conflicts. The inability to do so will either cause the business to fail or cause animosity among the various positions.

What is the first step?

Every business is different and the planning process must account for the uniqueness of each business. However, there are also similarities between businesses that allows for an effective process to be implemented.

The first step is to assemble the team of professionals that will be needed. While the talents needed on the advisory team will vary from business to business, virtually every teams needs a business attorney, a tax accountant, an insurance professional and a financial advisor who are experienced in creating successor plans. Bankers, investment bankers, business consultants, and other team members will be essential to some advisory teams.

What is the process of creating a Successor Plan?

In order to know where you are going, the first step is for the business owner, with the help of the advisory team, to identify the planning objectives. This includes such things as the amount of income the owner needs to maintain the owner's lifestyle, the projected date the owner intends to leave the business, and the most likely transferees of the business. Once the planning goals are known, the team will need to value the business and potentially help to increase the value of the business if more value is needed to meet the planning goals. If there are employees, they must be retained, and the adverse tax consequences of the succession plan must be minimized. The attorney will then draft the necessary business and estate planning documents that establish the agreed upon Plan.

Once the Plan has been formulated, it must be shared with the family. Dealing with potential conflicts among family members before the Plan is implemented will best ensure its success. If all the children know the Plan, and that the Plan was formulated by the parent, animosity against siblings is negated.

How long before retirement should the Plan be established?

For planning strategies to work to their maximum effect, it is important that the business owner and advisory team have time to work. It is best that the succession plan be conceptualized when the business is first created. If that is no longer possible, commencing work on the succession plan should not be further delayed. At a minimum, the design of a plan should commence at least five years before an anticipated departure of the owner from the business.

Remember, every business owner leaves the business at some point, whether the departure is voluntary or otherwise. The terms upon which the owner departs are determined by the planning that preceded the departure.

CHAPTER FOURTEEN

CHARITABLE PLANNING

No discussion of estate planning would be complete without considering the benefits of charitable planning. Such benefits include the possibility of making your philanthropic dreams come true, while at the same time reducing your taxes, gaining a more secure retirement, and even leaving more to your heirs than would otherwise be possible. If this sounds too good to be true, it is not. Charitable planning can truly create a win-win-win scenario for you, your favorite charities, and your heirs. For all these reasons, charitable planning is an important component of truly spectacular estate plans.

How can estate planning make my charitable dreams come true?

Many of our clients tell us that they want to use the opportunity of planning their estates to accomplish more than just leaving a windfall inheritance to their children—especially if the children are already financially independent. They inquire whether there is something else that can be done with their estates which will make a difference long after they are gone.

Perhaps like them you have yearned throughout your life for the opportunity to make this world a better place. Perhaps you have seen something that has struck your heart, and you want to help. Perhaps you have a deeply held desire to accomplish something that will outlive you. If so, your qualified estate planning can help you design and implement an estate plan that makes your philanthropic dreams come true.

If you have charitable goals that you want to see realized, the first step is to help the estate planning attorney understand the goals that you want to accomplish. The attorney's responsibility is to then help you explore your charitable planning options. Once your goals are set and your options explained, the two of you can design an estate plan that brings your dreams to fruition in a tax beneficial manner. By following these steps you can achieve truly extraordinary results.

What are my basic charitable planning options?

Your most basic charitable planning option is to simply make a charitable gift during your lifetime. There are several benefits to this type of gift. There is little or no planning cost. Also, since your gift is made during your life, you may be entitled to income tax deductions. Additionally, you get to see for yourself the joy that your gift brings to others.

A second basic charitable planning option available to you is to include a charitable bequest in your living trust or will. Following your death, the charity will receive its bequest and use it for the purpose designated by you. There are several benefits to this type of gift. The gift costs you nothing during your lifetime, other than the cost of including the bequest in your trust or will since it comes out of your estate only after your death. Also, your estate may be entitled to estate tax deductions. Additionally, your gift can create a legacy that helps to preserve the memory of you and your generosity.

Many people do not realize that even small charitable gifts made this way can accomplish great charitable objectives. These gifts can be easily made by anyone— even those who do not think of themselves as rich and never thought it possible that they could accomplish something great.

For example, even if you do not have the financial resources to make large charitable gifts during your lifetime, you can make a significant charitable impact by donating a percentage of your estate to any cause you want to promote. Even a charitable bequest of only 10% of most estates will make a huge difference.

Assume a couple has a $400,000.00 estate that consists of their home, retirement accounts, investments, savings, household possessions, and life insurance. Perhaps during their lives this couple was never in the financial position to make a significant charitable gift. But, if they simply include a 10% bequest to one or more charities among the beneficiaries named in their trust or will, the formerly impossible suddenly becomes possible.

Since the 10% charitable bequest will occur only after their deaths, it will not affect the couple's lifestyle at all. The remaining 90% of the estate will still be available for distribution to children and other beneficiaries—whose inheritance is barely impacted by the "small" charitable bequest! A 10% charitable gift made from a $400,000.00 estate will provide $40,000.00 to accomplish the couple's charitable goals, and that amount can make a significant difference in the world!

Many of our clients are proud of their ability to create a lasting legacy that will survive their deaths. They also like the idea of using their estate plan to teach their children that life is so much more than just "stuff." They understand that giving something back to the community can be one of life's most rewarding and fulfilling activities.

Clients are also surprised to learn that the charities they include in their estate plan may even desire to publically commend them during their lifetime. Charities believe that donors should be immediately recognized and applauded for their charitable generosity and vision, not just after they die. Donors are also pleased to learn that the tax code further rewards the charitably minded by providing several forms of tax relief.

When including charitable planning as part of your estate plan, you can achieve your philanthropic dreams, teach your children important life lessons, receive the thanks of a grateful charity, and possibly obtain significant tax benefits. Even basic charitable planning turns an ordinary estate plan into a truly superior one.

How does charitable planning provide tax benefits?

Any donation that you make to nonprofit charities is not subject to capital gain, income, or estate taxes. The amount of tax savings you receive depends on the following:

- The type of asset being donated;

- The charitable planning technique used;

- The amount of your annual income; and

- The size of your taxable estate.

When charitable planning is done right, the tax savings can be significant.

Whenever property or stock that has appreciated in value is sold, the federal government is poised to tax the profit (gain). This tax is known as a "capital gain tax" which siphons off a good portion of the money you receive from the sale of the asset. If you simply sell the assets and then donate the proceeds to the charity, two bad things happen. First, the amount of the charitable gift is reduced by the capital gain tax paid following the sale—the charity gets a smaller donation. Second, the income tax deduction to which you are entitled for your charitable generosity is also reduced. Instead of receiving an income tax deduction that is based on the full fair market value of the asset, the deduction received is the sale price of the asset minus the amount paid in capital gain tax—you get a smaller deduction. This is poor planning and there is a better way!

A better result is obtained if the asset is donated directly to the charity and then the charity sells the asset. No capital gain tax is paid because nonprofit charitable organizations are exempt from paying capital gain taxes! The charity wins because it receives a donation that equals the full sale price of the asset instead of one that is diminished by the payment of capital gain taxes. You also win because you receive a larger income tax deduction—one that is now equal to the full fair market value of the property. It is a classic win-win scenario.

Your lifetime gifts may also entitle you to income tax deductions. Factors affecting the income tax deduction include the value of the gift, the type of asset donated, and your reportable income. For example, you may receive larger tax deductions for cash gifts as opposed to gifts of appreciated property.

Estate tax deductions are available for gifts given after death. If you leave a donation to a charity through your living trust or will, your estate will receive a dollar for dollar reduction in the size of the estate. Because estate taxes are the highest rates in our taxing system, significant savings can be achieved through testamentary charitable gifts. The estate planning attorney can advise as to whether gifts from your estate would result in tax savings for you.

Are there even better charitable planning opportunities?

While direct charitable gifts provide wonderful results, even better opportunities are available if you implement more advanced planning utilizing a Charitable Trust.

What are Charitable Trusts?

A Charitable Trust is a special type of trust that is specifically designed to ensure that the assets held in the trust are exempt from estate and capital gain taxes. Preferential tax treatment is given to those who direct that the assets in the trust will someday be used for charitable purposes. There are two types of charitable trusts: Charitable Remainder Trusts and Charitable Lead Trusts. In both types of Charitable Trusts you can serve as the Trustee and control the investments and distributions of the trust assets and income.

What is a Charitable Remainder Trust?

A Charitable Remainder Trust (CRT) is a trust in which the trustmaker receives distributions from the trust during the trustmaker's lifetime, and the charitable beneficiaries get what is left when the trustmaker dies. The trustmaker selects the percentage of the trust assets the trustmaker will receive for either a number of years or the trustmaker's entire life, after which, the remaining trust assets are paid to the specified charities. The IRS has restrictions regarding the amount the trustmaker can take to ensure there is something left for the charity.

What is a Charitable Lead Trust?

Charitable Lead Trusts (CLT) differ from Charitable Remainder Trusts (CRT) with respect to the timing of the gift. With a CRT, the trustmaker receives the lifetime distributions and the charity receives the assets remaining at the time the trust terminates –which is usually at the death of the trustmaker or beneficiary. With a CLT the charity receives the lifetime distributions and the trustmaker (or the trustmaker's selected beneficiary) receives the assets remaining at the time the trust terminates. Recipients of income and assets are reversed with a CLT compared to a CRT.

Do additional charitable planning opportunities exist?

You can create "donor advised funds" with a local community foundation. This is accomplished by making your donation to the community foundation. The foundation handles the investments and distributions, although you can make suggestions as to who receives the distributions.

If you want to retain control over investments and distributions, you might want to consider creating your own charitable foundation. Having your own foundation provides your family greater control over the decision making process and can preserve your family's values and legacy across generations as children and then grandchildren are given the opportunity to serve on the foundation's board of directors. This can greatly enhance the standing and recognition of your family in the community as charitable organizations solicit grants from your foundation.

Although these charitable planning strategies provide some of the best opportunities, they are also among the most complex of the charitable strategies. They necessitate the assistance of experienced estate planning counsel skilled in charitable planning to ensure compliance with the many technical requirements of the tax code.

CHAPTER FIFTEEN

ESTATE ADMINISTRATION AFTER DEATH

A simple fact of life is that sooner or later we are all going to die, and at that time our estates will need to be administered. It is then that the surviving family will discover whether the estate has been well planned or poorly planned. Here are some of the benefits of a well-planned estate:

- The family will avoid probate court proceedings and all of its delays, costs, and loss of privacy;

- Your minor children will be cared for by the guardian you select;

- Your children's inheritance will be managed by those you trust;

- Estate taxes will be eliminated or minimized;

- Your beneficiaries will receive their inheritance when

you want and in the way you want;

- The inheritance will be protected from creditors, predators, and failed marriages; and

- Administration fees and costs will be minimized.

The pitfalls of a poorly planned estate include:

- Intrusive and expensive public court proceedings;

- Custody battles over your children;

- Your children's inheritance will be controlled by someone selected by a judge – not by you;

- Your family loses out on advantageous tax-planning opportunities;

- Unwanted heirs may receive the inheritance;

- Your loved ones receive their inheritance too soon or too late or receive too little or too much;

- The inheritance is not protected from creditors, predators, and failed marriages; and

- The estate unnecessarily pays higher professional fees and costs.

Will the administration of my estate receive the benefits of being well planned or suffer the consequences of being poorly planned?

The answer depends on which of the following five types of plans your estate matches:

1. You have done nothing.

2. You have planned with just joint tenancy, payable on death (POD) designations, or beneficiary designations.

3. You have planned with a will.

4. You have planned with an unfunded trust.

5. You have planned with a fully funded revocable living trust.

How will my estate be administered if I do nothing?

If you do no planning, you still have an estate that requires administration. The problem is that your estate will not be administrated according to your desires, but according to the government's default plan, which controls the estates of those who die without a plan of their own. The government's plan forces your estate into probate. The government's plan determines who gets custody of your children. The government's plan can leave your property to unintended heirs. The government's plan provides no protection from creditors, predators, and failed marriages. It also imposes the highest taxes and costs.

What if I plan with joint tenancy, POD designations, or beneficiary designations?

For small estates, joint tenancy, POD designations, and beneficiary designations might provide an efficient way to transfer property upon your death. These are cheap and easy ways to avoid probate, but there are many risks with this type of planning.

If you hold your property in joint tenancy with a child, you lose control. For example, your child can empty out the bank account, cash in the CDs, and sell all the stock. You will also lose the right to mortgage or sell your house without your child's permission. Additionally, your property will be subject to your child's creditors, lawsuits, and failed marriages. You might also be triggering unexpected gift- and capital gain tax consequences when you create joint tenancies.

Major problems also exist with POD and beneficiary designations. While you may use these strategies to avoid probate, such planning is not foolproof and may result in disastrous consequences. Assets subject to beneficiary designations or PODs will still need to be probated if your designated beneficiary dies before you do; if your beneficiary is a minor; or if your estate is named as the beneficiary. Also, payments made from POD and beneficiary designations directly to a disabled beneficiary may cause the beneficiary to lose his or her disability benefits. Leaving property to your children with these designations will expose it to your children's creditors, bankruptcies, and lawsuits. Beneficiary designations that are not kept up to date may pay to unintended heirs.

You must also remember that there are settlement costs and financial obligations for your estate to pay upon death. Attempting to arrange for a complete disposition of property by using POD, joint tenancy, or beneficiary designations may avoid probate, but it may also leave your Executor without any money to pay these debts, taxes, or expenses.

What if I plan with a will?

Since your will takes effect only at time of death, it is useless in the event of your disability.

Remember that wills also guarantee probate. Your family will receive its inheritance only after months or years of delay in the courts. In addition, the estate is subject to court costs and fees. Every beneficiary's inheritance will be made a public record. Wills are frequently contested and, in some cases, family members end up never speaking to each other again. Probate lawyers love wills.

What if I plan with an unfunded trust?

Property owned by a trust avoids probate, but remember that a trust controls only the property that it owns. If the trust owns nothing, it controls nothing. If the trust owns nothing (i.e., nothing is "funded" into the trust), the trust will not control the estate's property. In order to have a trust own and control property, it is necessary to re-title the asset (such as a deed to a house) so that the trust is named the new owner. Unfunded trusts require probate.

Many estates that utilize a revocable trust also include a

special will (known as a "pour over will"). The pour over will transfers any unfunded property to the trust when the owner dies, but this, too, requires probate. Now there are two administrations: first probate and then a trust administration. This adds delays and costs instead of preventing them. The pour-over will should be used only as a safety net to transfer unfunded property into the trust when a death occurs. The preferred way of planning is with a fully funded trust.

What if I plan with a fully funded trust?

This is the best way to plan. With a fully funded revocable living trust, all property owned by the trust will avoid probate and all its issues. This should lead to a smooth estate administration at the lowest cost and with the fewest delays.

How long will it take to administer my estate?

Well-planned estates take the least amount of time to administer. Unplanned or poorly planned estates will take much longer.

When you fail to plan or plan using a will, you must follow the mandates of your state's statutes, which are enforced by the Probate Court. When the Court takes charge, you lose control.

Before the administration process can start, an Executor must be named. Even if an Executor is named in your will, this person must be approved by your heirs or be appointed by the Probate Judge at a hearing. This may take weeks or months. Once an Executor has been appointed, a notice must be published in the newspaper giving creditors several weeks or months to file their claims. Generally, state law puts a time limit of 12 to 18 months to get the estate closed, but extensions are easily granted. There are many well-publicized estates that have taken years to resolve when there are disputes among the heirs or creditors.

The well-planned estate will be a trust-centered plan, which does not require court supervision. You name the trustee who takes charge immediately upon your death; no court appointment is required. Placing a notice in the newspaper for creditors is optional. Settlement proceeds at the pace controlled by the trustee. Because no court hearings or court approvals are required, smaller estates can frequently be settled within a few months. If estate taxes will be owed, trusts are usually kept open until the estate tax return is due, which is nine months after the date of death.

Why do unplanned or poorly planned estates take much longer?

- They cause court battles over who will represent the estate;

- They require protracted probate court proceedings with built-in delays (as discussed above);

- They make it easy for outsiders to file nuisance claims; and

- They set the stage for disgruntled heirs to challenge who gets the inheritance.

Any one of these things can cause lengthy delays. Fully funded revocable trusts avoid such delays for the following reasons:

- Your trust avoids probate court;

- Your trust names the person who will represent your estate, who can serve without obtaining court approval; and

- Your trust is a private document, which makes it difficult for outsiders to challenge its terms.

For all these reasons, planning with a fully funded trust will cause the least delay and burden to your loved ones.

How do attorneys charge for estate administration work?

Attorneys typically use one or a combination of three different methods. The first method is for the attorney to set an hourly fee and bill by the hour for the work that is performed. The second method is for the attorney to use a fixed percentage of the dollar value of the estate as the basis for the fee. The third method is for the attorney to quote a fixed fee that is based purely on the nature of the work that needs to be done. The method offered varies from state to state and from firm to firm.

How much will it cost?

Generally speaking, the more work that needs to be done, the more expense you can expect your estate to pay. As a general rule, the cost for administering an estate in the probate courts is about 3-8% of the total value of the estate. If you can avoid probate, you can avoid many of these costs. A fully funded revocable trust is one way to avoid probate and can result in significant savings even when the estate plan is relatively complex. You can expect to pay from 1% to 1.5% of the value of the estate for the administration of your trust, although it could be less. Your trustee will be paid as a part of your trust plan.

Do I need an attorney to administer my estate if it is fairly simple?

Yes, professional representation is always recommended in estate administrations. There simply is not enough room in this book to explain all of the possible issues that can occur in administering an estate. What may appear on its face to be a simple estate to administer may actually prove to be quite complex. Mistakes in estate administration can cost your family unnecessary time, taxes, and expenses.

Some of the benefits of working with an estate administration attorney include:

- Preparation of an inventory of the estate's assets, which is a listing of all of the estate's assets with date of death values;

- Determination of the new tax basis for the assets;

- Help to resolve claims against the estate;

- Help to select the best distribution options for life insurance, retirement plans, and annuities, as well as an explanation of the tax ramifications of those options;

- Tracking income and directing the preparation of fiduciary income tax returns for the estate and the final income tax return for the decedent;

- Preparation or revision of any estate tax returns that may be necessary;

- Keeping beneficiaries informed of progress;

- Assistance with distributions to the beneficiaries; and

- Help in preparation of the Final Account.

There are many complex decisions and a lot of work that must be done to administer even a "simple estate." Your estate administration attorney will help you negotiate the maze of technical issues and rules and regulations that must be followed to settle any estate.

CHAPTER 16

CHOOSING THE RIGHT ATTORNEY

There are many decisions that must be made at every step of the estate planning process, not to mention financial, legal, and tax implications that affect every one of those decisions. Due to the complexity of planning an estate, it is wise to seek expert help with making those decisions.

There is an adage in the law that he who represents himself has a fool for a client. This is especially true in the area of estate planning. We constantly see the devastating consequences of those who tried to plan their own estates. Often the surviving family is left with confusion, unnecessary taxes, and many other woes. Guardianship proceedings have to be filed that could have been avoided. Estates that could have escaped probate now have to undergo its costs, delays, and loss of family privacy. Family members get disinherited and unintended heirs get the inheritance. These and many other undesirable events frequently happen to the beneficiaries of those who try to do it themselves.

Even attorneys who practice in other areas of the law understand this and consult with estate planning attorneys when it comes time to plan their own estates. We humbly recommend that you follow their excellent example and obtain the help of a qualified estate planning attorney when it comes time to plan your estate.

What qualities should I look for in an estate planning attorney?

Finding a qualified estate planning attorney can be difficult. Some people use the yellow pages, which are full of ads, but tell you nothing of the quality of service you will receive. Some shop for price, but when it comes to obtaining quality estate planning services, as with most other things in life, you get what you pay for. Others rely on a general practice attorney who tries to do everything, but that is like going to your general practice doctor for heart surgery! Your family needs and deserves an attorney whose practice is devoted full-time to this special area of law.

How do I find the attorney my family needs and deserves?

In order to find the best estate planning attorney for you and your family, you need to be prepared to do a little investigation. Only attorneys who represent themselves as estate planning attorneys, and who are leaders in their fields, should be considered. Estate planning attorneys:

- Will be active members in prominent estate planning organizations and associations.

- Will have published articles and books on the subject of estate planning.

- Will be sought as speakers and teachers by other professional groups.

- Will be knowledgeable of the latest planning strategies and techniques through specialty continuing education.

Be willing to interview the attorney you are considering to determine if he or she meets the above criterion. The attorney should be willing to be interviewed by you without charge.

What interview questions should I ask?

The following interview questions are key to helping you choose the right attorney.

- *Will the attorney charge for the initial meeting?*

Most quality estate planning attorneys will provide a complimentary initial consultation. This gives you the opportunity to meet the attorney, check their qualifications, and develop a rapport before incurring a fee.

- *How does the attorney charge for his or her services?*

After working with you to design the estate plan that best accomplishes your goals, an experienced estate planning attorney will be able to determine the cost you will incur to create and implement the plan. Expect the attorney to quote an exact fee for the service to be provided.

Avoid attorneys who charge by the hour. They will tell you their hourly rate but rarely commit themselves to the number of hours that they will bill you. Such open-ended fee arrangements can result in the fee being much greater than you expected. Hourly fee arrangements do not promote attorney efficiency. We find that clients prefer to know the full cost up front rather than being surprised at the end with an unexpectedly large bill.

- *How long will it take?*

An experienced estate planning attorney should be able to have a comprehensive estate plan completed within approximately 30 days after being retained by the client to begin the work. You should expect the signing date to be scheduled at the time the attorney is retained.

- *What will you include in my estate plan?*

Your estate plan needs to be prepared to meet your specific needs. At a minimum, a comprehensive estate will include a revocable living trust, financial powers of attorney, health care directives, designation of guardians, and property agreements.

- *Will my plan avoid probate?*

The estates of those with no plan are probated! The estates of those who plan with only a will are probated! If you plan with a trust but fail to title your assets in the name of the trust, probate will be required! Since only fully funded revocable trusts avoid probate, retain only an attorney who will help you make sure that your trust is fully funded.

- *Will you help me fund my trust?*

Funding a trust means making it the owner or beneficiary of your property. Avoid attorneys who offer to draft your trust but do not assist in the funding process. A thorough estate planning attorney will offer to assist you in funding your trust.

- *How much time will you spend explaining my plan to me?*

Understanding your plan is critical. The right attorney will spend the time necessary explaining the complex documents to you in detail. This explanation will typically take one to two hours.

- *Do you offer a periodic review of my plan?*

Regular review of your plan is critical because of constantly changing family circumstances, new laws, and new planning strategies. The most dedicated attorneys are committed to keeping your estate plan up to date through periodic reviews.

- *Do you have your own revocable trust?*

A good estate planning attorney will have a trust to protect his or her own family. Avoid attorneys who do not personally believe in the services they provide to others.

- *Will my documents be organized in a portfolio?*

Be sure all your estate planning documents are assembled in logical order in a suitable binder with a table of contents. This will help you find what you are looking for in an emergency. It will ensure that all of your planning documents are together in one location. A well-organized portfolio will make it easier for your Trustee to understand and administer your estate.

We believe that attorneys who possess these characteristics and offer these services can best provide you with the quality estate planning services you and your family need and deserve.

Who else do I need to consult?

Estate planning involves reviewing your financial circumstances today to ensure that you are prepared for tomorrow. It requires that you and your attorney work with several other qualified professionals (including financial advisors, accountants, and insurance professionals) to ensure that you receive the best plan for your circumstances. For this reason, it is important that the attorney you select believes in working as part of an estate planning team of professionals and is capable of leading that team as it designs and implements your estate plan.

LEGACY EDUCATIONAL PUBLISHING MEMBER LIST

Sameer Chhabria
(312) 580-9500
300 Sanders Road
Riverwoods, IL 60015

Deborah B. Cole
(312) 786-2250
122 South Michigan Avenue
Suite 1220
Chicago, IL 60603-6263

Irene Clarke David
(847) 382-6620
18-6 East Dundee Rd
Suite 112
Barrington, IL 60010

William A. Deitch
(630) 871-8778
600 West Roosevelt Road
Suite A-1
Wheaton, IL 60187

Joseph P. Earley
(715) 246-7555
539 South Knowles Avenue
New Richmond, WI 54017

Kenneth M. Fleck
(262) 376-2222
7269 Highway 60
Cedarburg, WI 53012

Edward F. (Foss) Hooper
(800) 794-5548
(920) 993-0990
2 Systems Drive
Appleton, WI 54914

Howard M. Lang
(847) 367-4460
700 Florsheim Drive
Suite 11
Libertyville, IL 60048-3757

Andrew C. (Drew) MacDonald
(920) 560-4646
4650 West Spencer Street
Appleton, WI 54914-9106

Chris J. Mares
(920) 734-7000
2210 E. Evergreen Drive
Appleton, WI 54913

Ketra A. Mytich
(309) 673-1805
6809 North Knoxville Avenue
Suite B
Peoria, IL 61614-2812

Teresa Nuccio
(847) 823-9576
1460 Renaissance Drive
Suite 105
Park Ridge, IL 60068

Steven H. Peck
(847) 940-0607
300 Saunders Road
Riverwoods, IL 60015

Mark D. Perkins
(630) 665-2300
1751 S. Naperville Road
Suite 203
Wheaton, IL 60187

Chester M. Przybylo
(773) 631-2525
5339 N. Milwaukee Avenue
Chicago, IL 60630

Mark J. Rogers
(414) 289-9200
401 E. Kilbourn Avenue
Suite 400
Milwaukee, WI 53202

William R. Slate
(920) 398-2371
33 North Bridge Street
P.O. Box 400
Markesan, WI 53946

Wayne W. Wilson
(608) 833-4001
7633 Ganser Way
Suite 100
Madison, WI 53719

Robert P. Wolfson
(630) 778-7778
1555 Naperville/Wheaton Road
Suite 101
Naperville, IL 60563